LEVITICUS EXPLAINED

LEVITICUS EXPLAINED

Understanding the Book and Its Message for Today

Samuel Whitaker

Part of the Bible for Modern Life Series

Ascent Press

For those seeking clarity in the ancient words of Scripture.

CONTENTS

Disclaimer

This book provides an interpretive overview of the biblical text using historical scholarship and modern analysis tools. It is intended to help readers understand the themes, context, and message of the biblical narrative and is not intended to replace personal study of Scripture

Introduction

Why Leviticus Still Matters

Of all the books of the Bible, Leviticus is the one most readers intend to read and the fewest actually finish. Where Genesis pulls the reader forward with the momentum of origins and catastrophe, and Exodus with the drama of plagues and liberation and a mountain on fire, Leviticus stops the narrative almost entirely and replaces it with legislation. Sacrificial procedures. Priestly regulations. Purity codes governing what can be eaten, touched, and worn. Detailed instructions for the Day of Atonement. A calendar of feasts. A holiness code whose demands range from the structure of worship to the treatment of employees to the prohibition of revenge. For the reader who came to the Bible for a story, Leviticus can feel like arriving at a destination and finding a legal code where the landscape was supposed to be.

That disorientation is itself a clue to what Leviticus is doing. The book occupies the position it occupies in the Torah because the question it is answering is the question that the drama of Exodus made unavoidable: now what? Israel has been liberated from Egypt. The covenant has been ratified at Sinai. The tabernacle has been constructed according to precise divine specifications at the end of Exodus, and the glory of the LORD has filled it so completely that even Moses cannot enter. The God of Israel is now dwelling in the middle of the camp. And the question that this extraordinary fact immediately generates is not theological but practical: how do a finite, mortal, sinful people live in the immediate proximity of a holy God without being consumed by the holiness they are in the presence of? Leviticus is the answer. Every sacrifice, every purity regulation, every priestly procedure, every feast and fast in the book's twenty-seven chapters is part of the same sustained response to the same question.

This is why the rabbis of ancient Israel considered Leviticus the most important book of the Torah — the book with which children should begin their study of Scripture rather than ending it. Where modern readers tend to experience Leviticus as an obstacle between the excitement of Exodus and the resumed narrative of Numbers, the ancient tradition experienced it as the heart of the Torah's teaching: the place where the relationship between God and Israel is given its most specific and most practical shape. The relationship established in Genesis and dramatically enacted in Exodus requires, if it is to be sustained rather than merely celebrated, a set of practices and a way of life adequate to the character of the God with whom it has been established. Leviticus provides both.

For readers who come to Leviticus expecting the narrative momentum of the surrounding books, the experience requires a recalibration of what Scripture is for. Not all of it is story. Some of it is instruction — and the instruction is not supplementary to the story but its necessary extension. The God who liberated Israel from Egypt did not do so in order to leave Israel without guidance about what the liberated life requires. The same divine voice that spoke from the burning bush and parted the sea speaks in Leviticus from the newly constructed tabernacle, and the content of what it speaks is the detailed shape of the life that the covenant relationship makes both necessary and possible. Reading Leviticus well means receiving instruction as itself a form of grace — the grace of a God who does not simply set his people free and leave them to work out the implications on their own.

The specific instructions Leviticus contains are at once deeply strange to modern readers and more directly relevant than their strangeness initially suggests. The sacrificial system that occupies the first seven chapters describes practices that no Jewish community has observed since the Temple's destruction in 70 CE and that no Christian community has ever been required to practice. The purity codes of chapters eleven through fifteen govern conditions that most modern readers encounter only in medical contexts, if at all. The Year of Jubilee described in chapter twenty-five has never, so far as historians can determine, been consistently practiced by any society. And yet the theological logic that organizes every one of these specific instructions — the logic of holiness, atonement, restoration, and the relationship between divine character and human practice — addresses the most persistent questions of human existence as directly as any text in Scripture.

Leviticus was not written for scholars or for specialists in ancient Near Eastern religion. It was written for a community — a community that had just been constituted as the people of God through a series of events so dramatic that their descendants would be recounting them thousands of years later, and that now needed to know what being that people required of them in daily life. The question it answers is the question of every community that has entered a significant new relationship and discovered that the relationship has implications for how everything else is organized: how do we live in a way that corresponds to who we now are and whose presence we now inhabit? The chapters that follow explore the historical world that shaped Leviticus, the structure that organizes its argument, the major themes that run through its legislation, the ways it has been misread, and the specific ways it continues to address communities that take its claims seriously. The goal throughout is not to make Leviticus comfortable but to make it possible to receive it as the demanding, carefully organized, theologically serious document it is — one that has shaped the moral and religious imagination of more people across more centuries than most readers who skip it have any reason to suspect.

Chapter 1

The Human Question

"Be holy because I, the LORD your God, am holy."
— Leviticus 19:2 (NIV)

The Universal Sense That Something Must Be Addressed

Every serious human life eventually confronts the intuition that something stands between the person one is and the person one ought to be — or between the life one is living and the life that would be fully adequate to one's deepest sense of what is right and real. The specific form this intuition takes varies enormously across cultures and centuries. In some traditions, it surfaces as guilt — the awareness of specific wrongs committed that cannot be undone. In others, it appears as shame — the sense that one's fundamental condition is deficient rather than simply that one's actions have been wrong. In still others, it manifests as a generalized awareness of incompleteness, of having missed something essential, of being at a distance from whatever would constitute genuine flourishing. The content and the vocabulary differ. The underlying structure is consistent: something is not right, something needs to be addressed, and the resources available within ordinary life for addressing it are not adequate to the problem.

Leviticus begins with this intuition not as a psychological problem to be managed but as a theological fact to be taken seriously. The book opens in the immediate aftermath of the most extraordinary event in Israel's national memory: the glory of the LORD has filled the newly constructed tabernacle so completely that Moses himself cannot enter. The God of Israel is now present — genuinely, specifically, spatially present — in the middle of the camp. And this fact, which is simultaneously the fulfillment of everything Israel has been promised and the realization of the greatest gift any people could receive, is also immediately and acutely dangerous. The God whose glory fills the tabernacle is holy in a way that makes proximity to him a matter of life and death rather than simply a matter of religious preference. Something must address the gap between the holiness of the one who is present and the condition of the people in whose midst he has come to dwell.

Leviticus is the address. Every sacrifice it prescribes, every ritual it requires, every boundary it establishes between the clean and the unclean, every procedure it specifies for the priests who serve at the altar — all of it is organized around the single practical question that the glory filling the tabernacle made unavoidable: how does a people that is not holy maintain a relationship with a God who is? The ancient reader who approached Leviticus understood this question from the inside, as the organizing challenge of their communal life. The modern reader who approaches it from outside this framework must make the effort to inhabit the question before the book's answers can be received as anything more than antiquarian curiosity. The effort is worth making. The question Leviticus is answering is not an ancient question that the modern world has superseded. It is the question that every serious engagement with the reality of God eventually generates.

The Hunger for Genuine Access to the Sacred

Alongside the intuition that something must be addressed stands a second and equally persistent human hunger: the desire for genuine access to what is sacred — not the mere performance of religious activity but actual, substantive contact with the reality that religious activity points toward. This hunger is present in cultures that would not recognize the vocabulary of Leviticus as their own. The desire to be in the presence of something genuinely holy, to encounter a reality that is not diminished by one's approach to it, to belong to a community whose common life is organized around something genuinely transcendent rather than around the management of shared interests — this desire is not the exclusive property of the religious traditions that have named it most explicitly. It is a feature of human experience that surfaces in every culture that has taken seriously the possibility that the material world is not all there is.

Leviticus addresses this hunger with unusual specificity. The sacrificial system of the first seven chapters is not a set of arbitrary requirements imposed by divine fiat. It is a carefully organized system of approaches to the holy — ways of drawing near to the God who dwells in the tabernacle that are adequate to the character of the one being approached. The burnt offering, the grain offering, the fellowship offering, the sin offering, the guilt offering — each addresses a different dimension of the relationship between the worshipper and God, and each is designed to make genuine access possible rather than to substitute a religious performance for the real thing. The system as a whole is organized around the conviction that genuine access to the holy is possible and that the terms on which it is possible matter — that approaching a holy God in the wrong way is not merely theologically incorrect but genuinely dangerous, as the deaths of Aaron's sons Nadab and Abihu in chapter ten make devastatingly clear.

For modern readers formed in traditions that have inherited the New Testament's interpretation of the Levitical system as pointing toward and fulfilled in the sacrifice of Jesus, the sacrificial system of Leviticus can seem to have lost its direct relevance. But the hunger it was designed to address has not lost its relevance. The desire for genuine access to what is sacred — for a relationship with God that is not merely notional or cultural but genuinely transformative, organized around the actual character of the one being approached rather than around what is convenient for the one approaching — is as present in the contemporary moment as it has ever been. Leviticus addresses this desire by insisting that genuine access is possible and by specifying, with unusual precision, what genuine access requires.

The Question of What Holiness Requires in Practice

The declaration that stands at the center of Leviticus — be holy because I, the LORD your God, am holy — is among the most demanding and most misunderstood commands in the entire Bible. It is demanding because holiness in Leviticus is not primarily an interior disposition or a spiritual attainment but a comprehensive orientation of the whole life toward the character of God. It touches what is eaten and what is worn, and how fields are harvested and how employees are paid, and how disputes with neighbors are resolved, and how the vulnerable are treated, and how the land itself is used. The holiness code of chapters seventeen through twenty-six covers more dimensions of daily life than any other single section of the Torah, and its range is itself the argument: the God of Israel is not a deity whose claims are confined to what happens in religious contexts. His holiness is the standard for the whole of life, and the people who bear his name are called to embody that standard in every dimension of their common existence.

It is misunderstood because holiness is consistently read as a synonym for moral perfection — an impossible standard that functions primarily to reveal human inadequacy rather than to describe a genuinely attainable way of life. Leviticus does not treat holiness this way. The holiness it commends is not sinlessness but distinction — the visible difference between a people organized around the character and purposes of God and the peoples around them organized around other centers. The specific regulations of the holiness code are the shape this distinction takes in the concrete practices of daily life: the food laws that prevent Israel from simply absorbing the dietary practices of the surrounding cultures, the agricultural regulations that embody the conviction that the land belongs to God and is held in trust rather than owned outright, the sexual ethics that establish the boundaries within which the intimacy of the covenant community is sustained. Each regulation is a specific form of the same underlying call: to be visibly different in ways that correspond to the character of the God in whose name the difference is maintained.

The Longing for Restoration After Failure

Leviticus also addresses one of the most persistent and most painful features of human experience: the need for restoration after failure — for a way back into the relationship and the community from which one's actions have created distance. The sacrificial system is not primarily a system of punishment for sin. It is a system of restoration — a set of procedures by which the damage done to the relationship between a person and God, or between a person and the community, is addressed and the relationship is reconstituted. The sin offering and the guilt offering of chapters four through six are not designed to exact retribution for wrongdoing. They are designed to make restoration possible — to provide a mechanism by which the person who has sinned can be genuinely restored to the standing before God and the community that the sin has compromised.

The Day of Atonement described in chapter sixteen is the most concentrated expression of this restorative logic in the entire book. Once a year, the high priest enters the holy of holies — the only time in the year when this is permitted — and performs the elaborate rituals that address the accumulated sin of the entire

community. The two goats whose fates are determined by lot —
one sacrificed, one sent into the wilderness bearing the sins of the
people — enact in visible, physical, communal form the double
movement that genuine restoration requires: the address of the
sin's consequences and the removal of the sin itself. The Day of
Atonement is not primarily a day of fear and self-flagellation. It is
a day of genuine restoration — the annual reconstitution of the
relationship between God and his people that their inevitable
failures across the preceding year have compromised.

The longing for this kind of restoration — for a way back
that is genuine rather than merely formal, that addresses what has
actually been broken rather than simply declaring it irrelevant — is
one of the most persistent features of human experience in every
era. The mechanisms Leviticus provides for meeting this longing
are no longer operative in the form the book describes: the
Temple is gone, the priesthood is dispersed, the sacrificial system
has not been practiced in nearly two thousand years. But the
longing the system was designed to address has not diminished,
and the theological logic that organized the system — that
genuine restoration requires genuine address of what has been
broken, that the restoration is given by God rather than achieved
by human effort, that the community reconstituted by restoration
is the community that can sustain the holy life Leviticus
commends — continues to speak to every generation that takes it
seriously.

The Shape of What Follows

These dimensions — the universal sense that something must be
addressed between imperfect people and a holy God, the hunger
for genuine access to the sacred, the question of what holiness
requires in the texture of daily life, and the longing for restoration
after the failures that daily life inevitably produces — are not
separate topics that Leviticus handles in separate sections. They

are angles on a single claim that the book develops from its opening sacrifice to its closing covenant: that the God who is holy has made provision for a people who are not, that the provision is specific and sufficient, and that the life organized around it is not a burden but the shape of genuine flourishing for a people called to bear the name of the one in whose presence they dwell.

The chapters that follow examine the historical world that shaped Leviticus, the literary structure that organizes its argument, the major themes that run through its legislation, the ways it has been misread across centuries of engagement, and the specific ways it continues to address communities that take its claims seriously. The goal throughout is not to make Leviticus easier to receive but to make it possible to receive it more fully — to remove the obstacles that prevent a modern reader from engaging the text as the demanding, carefully organized, theologically serious document it is. Leviticus was not written as an obstacle to be endured before the more interesting parts of Scripture can be reached. It was written as instruction — the specific, practical, life-shaping instruction of a God who has drawn near and who takes seriously what nearness requires of the people in whose midst he has chosen to dwell.

Chapter 2

Orientation

"The LORD called to Moses and spoke to him from the tent of meeting."
— Leviticus 1:1

A Book for a Community at the Threshold

The historical circumstances that produced Leviticus are not background information to be acknowledged and set aside. They are the conditions that explain why the book sounds the way it does — why it opens not with narrative but with instruction, why its first word in the Hebrew is a calling rather than a declaration, why its entire concern is with how a specific people in a specific situation maintain a specific relationship with a specific God. Leviticus is a situational document. It was not written for all people in all times as a general account of religious philosophy. It was written for Israel at Sinai — a community camped at the foot of a mountain, organized around a newly constructed portable sanctuary, living in the immediate aftermath of the covenant ratification that had constituted them as the people of God, and navigating the daily practical question of what that constitution required of them in the conditions they were actually in.

The situation is unique in Israel's history, and the book's legislation is shaped at every level by its uniqueness. The tabernacle has just been completed. The glory of the LORD has just filled it. The sacrificial system the book prescribes presupposes a functioning sanctuary with a consecrated priesthood, a geographically concentrated community, and a set of agricultural practices that assume settlement in a specific land. Leviticus is the instruction manual for a way of life that does not yet fully exist at the moment the instruction is given — Israel is still in the wilderness, the land has not yet been entered, and the settled agricultural existence that many of the book's regulations presuppose is still a future prospect. This temporal tension is not a literary inconsistency. It is the formal expression of the book's fundamental conviction: that the shape of the life God requires of his people is given before the conditions in which that life will be fully lived are in place, because the law is not the product of the circumstances but the standard by which the circumstances are to be organized.

Authorship and the Mosaic Tradition

Leviticus does not identify its author within the text in the way that modern books identify their authors. The book presents itself consistently as the record of divine speech transmitted through Moses — the LORD called to Moses and spoke to him is the formula that introduces most of its major sections. The traditional attribution of the Torah as a whole, including Leviticus, to Moses has been the dominant view across most of Jewish and Christian history and remains the position of many readers and communities of faith today. Modern scholarship has approached the question of authorship differently, identifying within Leviticus the traces of what appears to be a priestly tradition — a body of material associated with the Aaronic priesthood and the concerns of the sanctuary — that was developed over a considerable period and reached something like its final form during or after the Babylonian exile of the sixth century BCE.

The question of compositional history, while genuinely interesting for understanding how the book came to take the form it has, does not determine the theological weight of its content. Whether Leviticus was composed in a single moment of Mosaic legislation or developed across centuries of priestly tradition, the theological claims it makes about the character of God, the nature of holiness, the mechanics of atonement, and the shape of the life that corresponds to covenant relationship are the claims that the book presents and that every reader must engage. The historical question of how those claims came to be formulated in the specific form they take is a legitimate scholarly question. The theological question of what they mean and what they require is the question that Leviticus presses on every reader who engages it seriously.

The Structure of the Book

Leviticus is organized into five recognizable sections that together cover the full range of the book's concerns. The sacrificial law of chapters one through seven establishes the procedures for the five major types of offering — the burnt offering, the grain offering, the fellowship offering, the sin offering, and the guilt offering — providing first the instructions for the worshippers and then the instructions for the priests. The ordination of the priesthood in chapters eight through ten narrates the installation of Aaron and his sons as Israel's priests, including the catastrophic episode of Nadab and Abihu whose unauthorized offering costs them their lives. The purity laws of chapters eleven through fifteen establish the boundaries between clean and unclean in the domains of food, bodily conditions, skin diseases, and household mold. The Day of Atonement in chapter sixteen stands at the structural center of the book and provides the annual mechanism for addressing the accumulated impurity and sin of the entire community. The holiness code of chapters seventeen through twenty-seven extends the concerns of the book into the full range of daily life — sexuality, agriculture, social ethics, the festivals calendar, the sabbatical and jubilee years, and the terms of the covenant that frames everything.

This structure is not simply organizational convenience. It is a theological argument pressed through arrangement. The book moves from the sanctuary outward — from the most concentrated point of divine presence at the altar, through the priestly mediation that makes access to that presence possible, through the purity regulations that maintain the conditions for approaching it, to the holiness code that extends the logic of the sanctuary into every dimension of daily life. The movement is centrifugal: holiness begins at the center, with the fire on the altar and the presence in the holy of holies, and radiates outward into the kitchen and the bedroom and the field and the marketplace. The entire book is the working out of what it means to live as a holy people in the presence of a holy God, pressed from the most explicit ritual contexts to the most ordinary practical ones.

Leviticus and the Ancient Near Eastern World

Leviticus did not emerge in a cultural vacuum. The ancient Near Eastern world in which it was composed was a world saturated with sacrifice, ritual purity, priestly institutions, and elaborate systems of approach to the divine. Mesopotamian and Egyptian religious texts describe sacrificial systems, purity regulations, and priestly procedures that share certain formal similarities with what Leviticus prescribes. This similarity is not evidence that Leviticus simply borrowed its content from the surrounding cultures. It is evidence that Leviticus was addressing questions — how do mortals approach the divine, what maintains the relationship between the human and the sacred, how is defilement addressed and purity restored — that every ancient culture in the region was also addressing, and that it was addressing them in a conceptual vocabulary that its original readers would have recognized.

What distinguishes Leviticus from the surrounding religious literature is not primarily the formal features of its ritual system but the theological convictions that organize it. The God of

Leviticus is not a deity who requires sacrifices because he needs them — he explicitly does not consume the food offered on the altar in the way that ancient Near Eastern deities were sometimes depicted as doing. The sacrifices are not bribes offered to an unpredictable divine power in order to secure favorable treatment. They are the God-given means by which a covenant relationship is maintained — the provision made by the holy God himself for the people he has called to live in his presence, given because the relationship requires them and because the God whose character they express has determined that such provision is what the relationship demands.

The Portrait of God in Leviticus

The portrait of God that Leviticus develops is the most concentrated portrayal of divine holiness in the entire Bible, and it is constructed through the book's sustained attention to the gap between divine holiness and human condition. The holiness of God in Leviticus is not primarily a moral category, though it has moral dimensions. It is an ontological one — a description of what God is in himself, the fundamental difference between the divine and everything that is not divine, the quality that makes proximity to God both the greatest gift and the most acute danger available to human beings. The fire that consumes the burnt offering when Aaron performs the inaugural sacrifices of chapter nine is not a supernatural special effect. It is the visible expression of the divine presence that has been the organizing reality of the entire book: holy fire, consuming what is offered, confirming that the approach to the holy has been made on terms adequate to the holiness being approached.

The deaths of Nadab and Abihu in chapter ten are the most disturbing episode in Leviticus and the most important for understanding the book's portrait of God. They offer unauthorized fire before the LORD — the text does not specify precisely what was wrong with it — and fire comes out from the presence of the LORD and consumes them. The episode is not presented as divine overreaction or as evidence of an arbitrary or unpredictable deity. It is presented as the natural and inevitable consequence of approaching a holy God in a way that does not correspond to the character of the one being approached. The holiness that makes genuine access possible is the same holiness that makes unauthorized access lethal, and the book's insistence on the precision of its ritual requirements is the formal expression of this conviction: getting it wrong is not a matter of religious fastidiousness. It is a matter of life and death.

The Role of the Priesthood

The Aaronic priesthood that Leviticus establishes and regulates occupies a position in the book's theological architecture that is impossible to overstate. The priests are the mediators — the figures whose specific calling is to stand between the holy God and the not-yet-holy people, to perform on the people's behalf the approaches to the divine presence that the people cannot make on their own terms, to maintain the conditions of the sanctuary that make the divine presence sustainable in the midst of the community. They are not simply religious professionals performing specialized functions. They are the structural solution to the fundamental problem that the book is organized around: how does a people that is not holy maintain a relationship with a God who is?

The ordination ceremony of chapters eight through ten is the most narratively developed section of Leviticus, and its narrative development is itself theologically significant. The installation of Aaron and his sons as Israel's priests is not a bureaucratic appointment. It is a transformation — a series of washings and anointings and sacrifices and the application of blood that changes the status of those who undergo it, setting them apart for a function that their birth alone would not have qualified them for. The priests are holy not because they are naturally different from the people they serve but because they have been made holy through a specific set of acts that the holy God has specified and that his servant Moses performs. Their holiness is not inherent. It is given — conferred by the same God whose holiness makes the conferral both necessary and possible.

Preparing to Read Leviticus Well

Understanding the historical situation of Leviticus — a community at Sinai, organized around a newly functioning sanctuary, receiving instruction for a way of life whose full conditions have not yet been established — the structure that moves from sanctuary outward into daily life, the ancient Near Eastern context that the book engages and transforms, the portrait of a God whose holiness is the organizing reality of every regulation the book contains, and the role of the priesthood as the structural mediation between the holy and the not-yet-holy: all of these are forms of orientation that prepare the reader to engage the text more fully.

But orientation is preparation, not replacement. The goal of everything this chapter has described is to clear away the obstacles that prevent a modern reader from engaging Leviticus directly — the sense that its ritual detail is arbitrary, that its purity regulations are primitive, that its priestly legislation is irrelevant to a post-Temple world. When those obstacles are cleared, what remains is the text itself: a carefully organized, theologically serious, pastorally attentive account of how a holy God makes provision for an unholy people to live in his presence. Leviticus rewards the reader who brings sufficient patience and sufficient theological seriousness to discover that the book is not, as it first appears, a detour from the biblical story. It is one of the story's most concentrated and most demanding movements — the moment when the God who liberated his people from Egypt turns to face them directly and asks: now that I am with you, how will you live?

Chapter 3

The World Behind the Book

"I am the LORD your God, who brought you out of Egypt, out of the land of slavery."
— Leviticus 11:45

The Wilderness Camp at Sinai

The world that produced Leviticus was, in the first instance, a camp — a large, organized, portable community living in the wilderness under conditions that were themselves theologically loaded. Israel at Sinai was neither the nomadic people it had been before Egypt nor the settled agricultural community it would become in Canaan. It was a people in between — liberated from one existence and not yet arrived at another, organized around the tabernacle that stood at the center of the camp and that gave the camp its reason for existing in the form it took. The layout of the camp was itself a theological statement: the tabernacle at the center, the Levites surrounding it as a buffer between the holy presence and the rest of the community, the twelve tribes arranged around the Levites in a specific order. The whole arrangement was a spatial enactment of the book's central concern: the holy is at the center, and the life of the entire community is organized in relation to it.

The wilderness setting also meant that Leviticus was given to a community without the agricultural infrastructure that many of its regulations assume. The land laws of chapters twenty-five — the sabbatical year and the Year of Jubilee — presuppose fields that have been farmed and owned for generations. The festival calendar of chapter twenty-three is organized around the rhythms of an agricultural year that Israel had not yet experienced in the land it was moving toward. The first-fruits offerings require harvests that had not yet been planted. This temporal gap between the giving of the law and the conditions for its full implementation is not an editorial problem. It is a theological feature: the shape of the life God requires is given before the situation in which it will be lived is established, so that the situation can be entered already knowing what fidelity to the covenant looks like within it.

The Ancient Near Eastern Sacrificial World

Israel's sacrificial system did not emerge into a world without sacrifice. The ancient Near East in the second millennium BCE was a world saturated with sacrificial practice — animals and grain and oil and incense offered to deities at temples and shrines across Mesopotamia, Syria, Canaan, and Egypt. The basic categories of Levitical sacrifice — the burnt offering consumed entirely on the altar, the communion meal shared between worshippers and deity, the sin offering addressing ritual impurity — have formal parallels in the religious literature and practice of Israel's neighbors. Ugaritic texts from ancient Canaan describe sacrificial terminology strikingly similar to Levitical vocabulary. Mesopotamian ritual texts prescribe procedures for approaching the divine that share the general logic, if not the specific content, of Levitical legislation.

Understanding this context is essential for avoiding two opposite misreadings of Leviticus. The first misreading treats the Levitical system as so uniquely revealed that it has no relationship to its cultural environment — a position that makes the formal similarities inexplicable and misses the genuine theological transformation the book performs on the materials it inherits. The second treats the similarities as evidence that Leviticus simply borrowed its system from the surrounding cultures — a position that misses the fundamental differences in theological conviction that distinguish Leviticus from every parallel text in the ancient world. Israel's God does not consume sacrifices because he is hungry. He does not require sacrifice to maintain his strength or secure his goodwill. He prescribes sacrifice because the relationship he has established with his people requires it — because the approach to the holy demands terms adequate to the holiness being approached, and because the gracious provision of those terms is itself an expression of the character of the God who makes them.

The Egyptian Background

Israel's experience in Egypt was not only the background against which the exodus was enacted. It was the formative context in which Israel's identity had been shaped for four hundred years, and its influence on the community that received Leviticus was pervasive in ways that the book itself addresses directly. Egypt was a world of elaborate priestly institutions, complex ritual purity systems, a sophisticated theology of the divine presence in temple sanctuaries, and an understanding of the relationship between the sacred and the ordinary that had organized Egyptian daily life for millennia. The Israelites who left Egypt had been formed by this world, had watched its priestly institutions function at close range, and carried its categories and assumptions with them into the wilderness.

The repeated formula that anchors Leviticus's identity claims — I am the LORD your God who brought you out of Egypt — is not merely historical reminiscence. It is the deliberate invocation of the founding event that constitutes Israel as a people and establishes the authority of the legislation that follows. The God who gives these instructions is not an abstract deity whose authority rests on general metaphysical claims. He is the specific God who performed specific acts in a specific historical context that the people receiving these instructions witnessed or inherited. The legislation of Leviticus is given within the covenant relationship that the exodus established, and the exodus remains the reference point that gives the legislation its context and its claim on the people who receive it.

The Canaanite Religious Landscape

Israel was moving toward a land already inhabited by peoples whose religious practices were well established and whose appeal to a newly arrived, semi-nomadic community would be significant. The Canaanite religious world was organized around the worship of Baal and Asherah and a pantheon of other deities whose cults were embedded in the agricultural landscape — in the high places on the hilltops, in the sacred groves, in the fertility rituals that organized the planting and harvest seasons. These practices were not simply different from what Leviticus prescribes. Many of them were specifically condemned by it, and the condemnations are not arbitrary prohibitions against foreign customs. They are targeted rejections of practices whose theological logic was incompatible with the character of Israel's God and the nature of Israel's covenant relationship with him.

The sexual regulations of Leviticus eighteen, which modern readers often find the most difficult section of the book to engage, are explicitly framed as the rejection of what the Egyptians practiced and what the Canaanites practiced — the practices of the peoples on whose land Israel is about to settle. The framing is not xenophobic. It is theological: the boundaries that Leviticus establishes around sexual life are the boundaries appropriate to a people whose identity is defined by their relationship to a holy God rather than by the religious practices of their neighbors. The land itself is described in chapter eighteen as having been defiled by the practices of its previous inhabitants — a claim that extends the logic of purity from persons and sanctuaries to the physical landscape, and that gives Israel's entry into the land the character of a restoration rather than simply a conquest.

The Social World of Clan and Tribe

The social world that Leviticus addresses is organized around the extended family — the household and the clan rather than the individual and the nuclear family. Property in the ancient Israelite world was primarily a family possession, transmitted across generations and defining the economic and social standing of every member of the family unit. Marriage alliances organized clan relationships. The redemption of kin — the responsibility of relatives to purchase back family members who had fallen into debt slavery or to redeem property that economic misfortune had forced the family to sell — was a fundamental social institution that the book of Ruth illustrates in narrative and that Leviticus legislates in the regulations of chapter twenty-five.

This social context is directly relevant to some of Leviticus's most distinctive legislation. The Year of Jubilee in chapter twenty-five — the fiftieth year in which all land reverts to its original family and all debt slaves are freed — is not a utopian fantasy disconnected from the social realities of ancient Israel. It is a specific legislative response to the dynamics of a clan-based agricultural economy in which the concentration of land ownership through debt was a real and persistent threat to the social fabric that the covenant community required. The theological grounding of the Jubilee — the land is mine and you are but aliens and my tenants — is not simply a religious rationale for an economic regulation. It is the foundational claim that organizes the entire economic ethic of Leviticus: the resources that human communities manage belong ultimately to God, and the arrangements by which those resources are distributed must reflect his character and his purposes rather than simply the outcomes of unconstrained market forces.

A World Defined by the Boundary Between Sacred and Ordinary

The world behind Leviticus is finally a world in which the boundary between the sacred and the ordinary is the most significant boundary in existence — more significant than the boundaries between nations, between social classes, between the wealthy and the poor. The distinction between holy and common, between clean and unclean, that runs through every section of the book is not a primitive superstition to be explained away by modern anthropology. It is the formal expression of a fundamental theological conviction: that God is genuinely present in the world, that his presence is genuinely holy, and that the approach to holiness requires genuine attention to the conditions of that approach.

The purity system of chapters eleven through fifteen is the most frequently misread section of this world in modern reception. The conditions it designates as unclean — certain foods, certain bodily discharges, certain skin conditions, certain states associated with death — are not moral failures or signs of divine disfavor. They are conditions that, for reasons the text does not always make explicit, are incompatible with approach to the sanctuary. The system is not primarily about hygiene, though some of its regulations may have hygienic dimensions. It is about the management of the boundary between the ordinary and the holy — the maintenance of the conditions under which genuine approach to the divine presence is possible. The world Leviticus describes is a world in which that boundary matters enough to be the organizing principle of daily life, and the book that manages it is the book Israel needed most precisely because the God in whose presence they were living was genuinely, specifically, and consequentially holy.

Chapter 4

The Story or Flow of the Book

"Aaron lifted his hands toward the people and blessed them. And having sacrificed the sin offering, the burnt offering and the fellowship offering, he stepped down."
— Leviticus 9:22

The Shape of Leviticus

Leviticus does not unfold as a story in the conventional sense. There is no protagonist whose journey organizes the narrative, no dramatic conflict whose resolution drives the reader forward, no sequence of events building toward a climactic moment. What Leviticus has instead of narrative momentum is legislative architecture — a carefully ordered arrangement of instruction that moves from the most specific and concrete requirements of the sanctuary cult outward through progressively wider circles of the community's life until the entire scope of the covenant relationship has been addressed. Reading Leviticus well requires learning to follow an argument pressed through legislation rather than through story, to recognize that the arrangement of the material is itself doing theological work, and to attend to what the placement of each section within the whole reveals about the convictions organizing the whole.

The overall movement of the book is centrifugal: it begins at the altar — the most concentrated point of divine-human encounter — and moves outward through the priestly mediation that makes the altar accessible, through the purity regulations that maintain the conditions for approach, to the holiness code that extends the logic of the sanctuary into the full range of daily life. This movement is not simply organizational convenience. It is the formal expression of the book's central theological argument: that holiness begins at the center, with the presence of the holy God in the sanctuary, and radiates outward from that center into every dimension of the community's existence. The book ends not where it began, at the altar, but in the fields and marketplaces and households of the community — which is precisely where the holiness the altar represents is meant to be lived out.

The Sacrificial Law

The first seven chapters of Leviticus establish the procedures for the five major types of offering that will organize Israel's worship at the sanctuary. The burnt offering of chapter one is the most basic and most comprehensive: the entire animal is consumed on the altar, nothing is retained for the worshipper or the priest, and the offering is described as an aroma pleasing to the LORD. The comprehensiveness of the burnt offering — its complete dedication to God without remainder — establishes the theological logic that the subsequent offerings will develop from different angles. Worship in Leviticus is not primarily about what the worshipper receives. It is about what the worshipper brings and what the bringing means.

The grain offering of chapter two and the fellowship offering of chapter three introduce the communal dimension of Levitical worship. The grain offering is the contribution of the agricultural worker — the first fruits of the field presented to the God who gave the field its fertility. The fellowship offering, whose meat is shared between the altar, the priests, and the worshippers, is the sacrifice of celebration and communion — the meal that expresses the relational character of the covenant in its most basic social form. These offerings establish that worship in Leviticus is not exclusively a transaction between an individual and God. It is a communal practice whose forms embody the character of the relationship between the whole people and the God in whose presence they live.

The sin offering of chapter four and the guilt offering of chapter five introduce the most theologically consequential dimension of the sacrificial system: the provision for addressing failure within the covenant relationship. The sin offering covers inadvertent violations of the law — wrongs committed without full awareness or intention. Its provisions are carefully calibrated to the social position of the offender: different requirements for the anointed priest, for the whole community, for a leader, and for an ordinary member of the community. The distinction reflects a conviction that runs through the entire book: greater access to the holy carries greater responsibility for maintaining the conditions that the holy requires. The guilt offering addresses cases where the violation has created a concrete material deficit — where something has been wrongfully taken or withheld — and requires restitution plus a penalty as the condition for genuine restoration.

The Ordination Narrative

Chapters eight through ten are the most narratively developed section of Leviticus and the most emotionally charged. The ordination of Aaron and his sons as Israel's priests — narrated across chapters eight and nine — follows a precise sequence that Moses performs exactly as the LORD commanded: washing, robing, anointing, sacrifice, the application of blood to the right ear and the right thumb and the right big toe of each priest. The precision is not ceremonial fastidiousness. It is the enactment of the conviction that the approach to the holy must correspond to the terms the holy God has specified, and that Moses's exact compliance is the condition on which the ordination's validity rests.

The climax of the ordination narrative in chapter nine is one of the most dramatic moments in all of Torah. Aaron performs his first official sacrifices as high priest. Moses and Aaron go into the tent of meeting and come out and bless the people. And the glory of the LORD appears to all the people, and fire comes out from the presence of the LORD and consumes the burnt offering and the fat portions on the altar. The people see it. They shout. They fall face down. The divine acceptance of the sacrifice is not a private spiritual transaction. It is a public, visible, communal event — the confirmation that the system of approach the first seven chapters established is real, that genuine access to the holy is possible, and that the God who specified the terms of approach actually receives what is offered on those terms.

The account of Nadab and Abihu in chapter ten is the necessary dark counterpart to the glory of chapter nine. Aaron's two eldest sons offer unauthorized fire before the LORD — the text says they offered strange fire that he had not commanded — and fire comes out from the presence of the LORD and devours them. The juxtaposition with the preceding chapter is deliberate and jarring: the same divine fire that confirmed the valid offering destroys the invalid one. Moses's explanation to Aaron — among those who approach me I will show myself holy; in the sight of all the people I will be honored — is the book's most concentrated statement of the principle that the entire sacrificial system embodies. The holy is not manageable. It cannot be approached casually or creatively. The terms matter, and the consequences of ignoring them are real.

The Purity Laws

Chapters eleven through fifteen address the boundaries between clean and unclean across four domains: food, bodily discharges, skin conditions, and household contamination. The food laws of chapter eleven are the most familiar section of Leviticus to modern readers, partly because their influence on Jewish dietary practice has been so pervasive and partly because they have generated so much interpretive controversy about the principle underlying their specific distinctions. Animals that chew the cud and have split hooves are clean; those that do one but not the other are not. Water creatures with fins and scales are clean; those without are not. The specific logic of these distinctions has been debated across centuries, with proposals ranging from the hygienic to the symbolic to the structural. What is clear is that the distinctions are real and consequential, and that their consistent observance is presented as a dimension of the holiness that distinguishes Israel from the surrounding nations.

The regulations governing bodily discharges in chapters twelve through fifteen address conditions that modern readers tend to find the most alien section of the book. Childbirth, skin conditions, bodily discharges of various kinds — all of these are subject to regulations specifying periods of impurity, procedures for purification, and offerings to be presented at the conclusion of the impurity period. The critical interpretive point is that impurity in these chapters is not sin and is not moral failure. A woman who has given birth is not being penalized for the birth. A man with a skin disease is not being punished for sin. The impurity associated with these conditions is a liturgical category — a designation of incompatibility with approach to the sanctuary — rather than a moral verdict on the person in whom the condition occurs. The purification procedures provide the mechanism for restoring the capacity for sanctuary approach, not the mechanism for moral rehabilitation.

The Day of Atonement

Chapter sixteen stands at the structural and theological center of Leviticus and is the most important single chapter in the book. The Day of Atonement — Yom Kippur in Hebrew, a name that means the Day of Covering or the Day of Wiping Clean — is the annual provision for addressing the accumulated impurity and sin of the entire community, including the accumulated impurity of the sanctuary itself. Aaron enters the holy of holies — the only time in the year when this is permitted — in simple linen garments rather than the elaborate high priestly vestments, a detail that emphasizes the gravity and the vulnerability of the moment. He performs sacrifices for himself and his household first, because a high priest who has not been cleansed cannot cleanse anyone else.

The two goats whose fates are determined by lot are the most memorable image in the chapter. One goat is sacrificed as a sin offering. The other — the scapegoat, in the original meaning of that word — has the sins of the entire community confessed over it by Aaron and is then sent into the wilderness bearing those sins away. The two animals enact the double movement that genuine atonement requires: the address of sin's consequences through sacrifice, and the removal of sin itself through the symbolic sending away. The Day of Atonement is not a day of fear in the primary sense. It is a day of genuine, comprehensive, communal restoration — the annual reconstitution of the covenant relationship that the community's inevitable failures across the preceding year have compromised.

The Holiness Code and the Meaning of the Whole

The holiness code of chapters seventeen through twenty-seven is the most extensive and most practically ambitious section of Leviticus, and its scope is itself the argument. The command to be holy because the LORD your God is holy is extended here into domains that have no obvious connection to the sanctuary: the prohibition of eating blood, the sexual ethics of chapter eighteen, the social ethics of chapter nineteen — which contains within a few verses the commands to honor parents, observe the Sabbath, leave the edges of fields unharvested for the poor, pay workers promptly, judge fairly, and love the neighbor as oneself — the penal regulations of chapter twenty, the special holiness requirements for priests, the festival calendar, the lamp and bread regulations for the sanctuary, the sabbatical and jubilee years, and the covenant blessings and curses of chapter twenty-six.

Reading the holiness code as a whole reveals the argument that Leviticus has been building across its entire length. The holiness that begins at the altar does not stay at the altar. The God who is present in the sanctuary is present in the community, and the community that lives in his presence must organize its entire existence — its eating and its sexuality and its agricultural practices and its treatment of the poor and its legal institutions and its management of the land — in correspondence to the character of the one in whose presence it lives. The holiness code is the most comprehensive statement in Scripture of what it means to be a holy people in a holy land under a holy God, and its scope is the measure of the seriousness with which Leviticus takes that calling. The book does not end at the altar. It ends in the fields and the households and the courts of the community — which is precisely where holiness is meant to be practiced and where the covenant relationship is either honored or abandoned in the texture of daily life.

Chapter 5

Key Themes

"Be holy because I, the LORD your God, am holy."
— Leviticus 19:2

Holiness

No theme is more central to Leviticus than holiness, and no theme in the book is more consistently misunderstood by modern readers. Holiness in contemporary usage has been reduced almost entirely to a moral category — the quality of a life free from major ethical failure, the condition of a person whose behavior meets a high religious standard. This reduction, while not entirely wrong, is profoundly inadequate to what holiness means in Leviticus. The Hebrew word translated holy — qadosh — carries the primary sense of separateness or distinction: to be holy is to be set apart, differentiated from the ordinary, dedicated to a purpose that the ordinary does not serve. When Leviticus declares that God is holy, it is not primarily saying that God meets a high ethical standard. It is saying that God is fundamentally, categorically, ontologically different from everything that is not God — that the distance between the divine and the creaturely is not a difference of degree but a difference of kind.

This understanding of holiness as fundamental distinction rather than primarily moral excellence shapes everything Leviticus requires. The sacrifices are holy because they are set apart from ordinary use and dedicated to the service of the sanctuary. The priests are holy because they are set apart from the general population for the specific function of mediating between the holy God and the not-yet-holy people. The Sabbath is holy because it is set apart from the ordinary working days of the week as a day whose character is determined by the God who rested on the seventh day of creation. The festivals are holy because they are set apart from ordinary time as occasions whose significance is determined by the events in Israel's history that they commemorate and whose observance constitutes a form of participation in those events across every subsequent generation. In each case, holiness is conferred by dedication — by the act of setting something apart from the ordinary for the service of the holy God.

The command to be holy because the LORD your God is holy — repeated across Leviticus and reaching its most extended development in the holiness code of chapters seventeen through twenty-seven — is therefore a command to embody in the community's life the same quality of distinction that characterizes God's own being. Not to be divine, which is impossible, but to be visibly and consistently different from the peoples and cultures around Israel in ways that correspond to the character of the God in whose name that difference is maintained. This is why the holiness code moves so readily between what appear to be religious requirements and what appear to be ethical ones: the commands to observe the Sabbath, to honor parents, to leave field edges for the poor, to pay workers on time, to judge fairly, to love the neighbor as oneself are all expressions of the same holiness, because holiness in Leviticus is not confined to the sanctuary. It is the character of the entire life of the people who bear the name of the holy God.

Atonement

The concept of atonement — the covering or wiping away of sin and impurity so that the relationship between the offender and God can be restored — is the theological engine that drives the entire sacrificial system of Leviticus. The Hebrew word translated atonement — kipper — appears more frequently in Leviticus than in any other book of the Bible, and its repeated use is not rhetorical habit but theological precision. Atonement in Leviticus is not primarily a legal transaction in which a penalty is paid by a substitute so that justice can be satisfied. It is a relational restoration — the addressing of whatever has compromised the covenant relationship so that the relationship can be reconstituted and the people can continue to live in the presence of the holy God without being destroyed by the unaddressed gap between their condition and his.

The mechanics of atonement in Leviticus are specific and varied. The burnt offering atones through the complete dedication of the animal to God — the worshipper's total self-offering expressed in the consuming of the entire sacrifice on the altar. The sin offering atones by addressing inadvertent violations of the law through a graduated series of sacrifices calibrated to the social position of the offender. The guilt offering atones by combining sacrifice with restitution, addressing cases where the violation has produced a concrete material deficit that must be made good before the sacrificial address is complete. The Day of Atonement atones comprehensively — covering the accumulated sin and impurity of the entire community and the sanctuary itself through the elaborate rituals that chapter sixteen prescribes. Each form of atonement is appropriate to its specific context, and the range of mechanisms the book provides reflects the conviction that the covenant relationship is robust enough to sustain multiple forms of failure and capacious enough to require multiple forms of address.

The blood of the sacrifice is the specific instrument of atonement in Leviticus, and its role is explained explicitly in chapter seventeen: the life of a creature is in the blood, and I have given it to you to make atonement for yourselves on the altar; it is the blood that makes atonement for one's life. This explanation is crucial for understanding why blood appears so pervasively in the book's ritual prescriptions. Blood is not a magical substance whose application produces automatic results. It is the bearer of life, and its use in the atonement rituals is the formal expression of the principle that genuine restoration of the relationship with the God of life requires the giving of life — not the worshipper's own life, which the sacrificial system is designed to make unnecessary, but the life of a creature offered in the worshipper's place on terms that the holy God has himself specified.

Clean and Unclean

The distinction between clean and unclean that runs through Leviticus eleven through fifteen and surfaces repeatedly throughout the holiness code is one of the most conceptually foreign features of the book for modern readers, and one of the most important for understanding what the book is doing. Clean and unclean are liturgical categories — designations of suitability or unsuitability for approach to the sanctuary — rather than moral categories designating good and evil. A woman who has given birth is unclean; she has done nothing wrong. A man who has touched a corpse is unclean; the contact may have been an act of love or duty. A person with a skin disease is unclean; the condition is not a punishment. In each case, the uncleanness is a temporary liturgical status that the book's purification procedures are designed to address, not a verdict on the moral character of the person in whom it occurs.

Understanding this distinction protects against the moralistic misreading of the purity laws that has caused so much damage in the history of their reception — the reading that treats the conditions designated as unclean as shameful, that uses the language of purity to stigmatize the people in whom those conditions occur, that extracts the book's liturgical categories from their specific context and applies them as general moral verdicts on conditions that the book itself treats as temporary and resolvable. The purity system of Leviticus is a system of boundaries — carefully maintained distinctions between conditions that permit sanctuary approach and conditions that do not — and those boundaries serve the purpose of making genuine access to the holy possible rather than the purpose of dividing people into the worthy and the unworthy.

The purity system also reflects a coherent symbolic logic that modern interpreters have identified in various ways. The food laws distinguish between creatures that fit clearly within the categories of their domain — land animals that chew the cud and have split hooves, water creatures with fins and scales — and those that do not. The bodily impurity regulations cluster around conditions associated with the boundaries of life — birth, death, disease, the bodily processes most directly connected to the generation and sustaining of life. Whether the specific logic of these distinctions is primarily hygienic, symbolic, or structural remains debated. What is clear is that the system as a whole is organized around the conviction that the boundary between the holy and the ordinary must be actively maintained, that the conditions for approach to the sanctuary matter, and that the provision for addressing impurity is itself a form of grace — the divine provision of a way back to the conditions that make genuine encounter with the holy possible.

The Priesthood as Mediator

The Aaronic priesthood that Leviticus establishes and regulates is not simply an administrative institution created to manage the sanctuary's operations. It is the structural solution to the book's organizing theological problem: the gap between the holiness of the God who dwells in the tabernacle and the condition of the people in whose midst he dwells. The priests stand at the boundary — between the holy of holies and the holy place, between the holy place and the outer court, between the sanctuary and the camp — and their function is precisely to mediate across those boundaries on behalf of the people who cannot cross them on their own terms.

The demands placed on the priesthood in Leviticus are more extensive and more rigorous than the demands placed on ordinary Israelites, and the extension of rigor is itself theologically significant. Greater proximity to the holy entails greater responsibility for maintaining the conditions the holy requires. The priests must avoid contact with corpses more carefully than ordinary Israelites. They must marry within specific boundaries. They must be free from certain physical blemishes that would compromise their fitness to serve at the altar. They must maintain the specific purity standards that their proximity to the sanctuary demands. These requirements are not arbitrary restrictions on priestly freedom. They are the formal expression of the principle that the closer one stands to the holy, the more completely one's life must correspond to its requirements — a principle that the deaths of Nadab and Abihu demonstrate in its most extreme form and that the detailed priestly regulations elaborate in its more ordinary dimensions.

The high priest's unique role is the most concentrated expression of the mediatorial function. He alone enters the holy of holies. He alone performs the Day of Atonement rituals that address the accumulated sin of the entire community. He bears the names of the twelve tribes on his breastplate when he enters the sanctuary, carrying the community into the divine presence in a form that the community cannot enter on its own. The vestments he wears — described in elaborate detail in Exodus twenty-eight and referenced throughout Leviticus — are themselves a theological statement: the high priest who enters the presence of the holy God wears garments whose composition and construction correspond to the character and the purposes of the one whose presence he is entering. The priesthood in Leviticus is not simply a religious bureaucracy. It is the embodied institution of the conviction that genuine access to the holy is possible and that God has provided the means for it.

Sacred Time and the Festivals

Leviticus twenty-three provides the most comprehensive festival calendar in the Torah, listing the seven appointed feasts whose observance structures Israel's sacred time across the year: the Sabbath, Passover and Unleavened Bread, Firstfruits, the Feast of Weeks, the Feast of Trumpets, the Day of Atonement, and the Feast of Tabernacles. The calendar is not simply a religious schedule. It is a theology of time — a declaration that time itself, like space and persons and animals and grain, can be set apart for holy purposes, and that the regular return to these appointed occasions is one of the primary means by which Israel maintains its identity as the people of God across the generations.

Each festival commemorates a specific dimension of Israel's relationship with God and enacts a specific aspect of that relationship in the present. Passover commemorates the exodus and enacts, in the annual meal whose preparation and consumption are carefully specified, the community's participation in the defining event of its constitution as a people. The Feast of Weeks commemorates the giving of the Torah at Sinai and presents the firstfruits of the wheat harvest — the offering of the first and best of the agricultural year to the God who gave the land its fertility. The Feast of Tabernacles commemorates the wilderness wandering and enacts, in the booths that Israelites are commanded to construct and live in for seven days, the memory of the condition from which God's provision sustained them. The festivals are not simply commemorations of the past. They are the liturgical practices by which the past's significance is made present and the community's identity is renewed across every subsequent generation.

The Sabbath that stands at the head of the festival calendar is the most fundamental unit of sacred time in Leviticus and in the Torah as a whole. Its observance is grounded not in agricultural utility or social convention but in the character of God himself — the God who rested on the seventh day of creation and who commands his people to rest as a participation in the divine rest. The Sabbath is the weekly declaration that the community's life is not organized primarily around economic productivity or the management of survival but around the God whose own life includes rest and whose people are called to embody that rest as part of their distinctive identity. The sabbatical year and the Year of Jubilee extend the logic of the weekly Sabbath into the rhythms of the agricultural calendar, declaring that the land itself participates in the rest that the covenant community is called to practice and that the economic arrangements of the community must reflect the character of the God who commands the rest.

The Land and the Jubilee

The theology of the land in Leviticus is one of the book's most distinctive and most practically consequential contributions to the biblical canon. The land is not simply the territory in which Israel will live after the conquest of Canaan. It is a theological actor — a party to the covenant whose treatment reflects the character of the covenant relationship and whose conditions respond to the faithfulness or unfaithfulness of the people who inhabit it. Chapter eighteen explicitly describes the land as having been defiled by the practices of its previous inhabitants and as having vomited them out as a consequence. Chapter twenty-six warns that continued disobedience will result in the land vomiting Israel out in the same way. The land has a moral sensitivity, in Leviticus's theological framework, that corresponds to the holiness requirements of the God who owns it.

The sabbatical year and the Year of Jubilee in chapter twenty-five are the most direct expressions of this theology. Every seventh year, the land is to lie fallow — not planted, not pruned, not harvested in the ordinary way. Whatever grows of itself is available to the poor and to the animals, but the agricultural economy of cultivation and harvest is suspended. The theological grounding is the same as the Sabbath: the land belongs to God, and the acknowledgment of his ownership is expressed in the periodic suspension of the human management of it. The sabbatical year is not primarily an agronomic practice, though it may have agronomic benefits. It is a theological practice — the regular, embodied acknowledgment that the land and its productivity are gifts held in trust rather than resources owned outright.

The Year of Jubilee — the fiftieth year, following seven cycles of seven sabbatical years — extends the logic further into the economic arrangements of the community. In the Jubilee, all land that has been sold reverts to its original family, and all Israelites who have sold themselves into debt slavery are freed. The economic logic of the Jubilee is the direct consequence of the theological claim that undergirds the sabbatical year: because the land belongs to God and Israel is his tenant, no permanent alienation of the land from the family to whom God assigned it is legitimate. The Jubilee is the built-in corrective to the inevitable concentration of land ownership through debt that a market economy left to its own logic would produce, and its theological foundation — you cannot ultimately own what belongs to God — is among the most radical economic claims in the entire biblical tradition.

The Covenant Blessings and Curses

The book of Leviticus concludes in chapter twenty-six with the most extensive statement of covenant consequences in the entire book — a passage whose formal structure echoes the suzerainty treaties of the ancient Near East, in which a great king would specify the blessings his vassals could expect for faithful loyalty and the curses they could expect for rebellion. The blessings promised for obedience are specific and concrete: rain in its season, abundant harvests, peace in the land, victory over enemies, and above all the continuation of the divine presence — I will walk among you and be your God, and you will be my people. The curses threatened for disobedience are equally specific and progressively intensifying: disease, drought, defeat by enemies, the terror of exile, and ultimately the desolation of the land and the scattering of the people among the nations.

The covenant blessings and curses of chapter twenty-six are not primarily a motivational device — a carrot-and-stick arrangement designed to secure compliance through the prospect of reward and punishment. They are a theological claim about the relationship between the community's faithfulness to the covenant and the conditions of its life in the land. The covenant relationship is not a private spiritual arrangement between God and individual souls. It is a public, material, historically consequential relationship between God and a community, and the conditions of that community's common life reflect the quality of its engagement with the covenant. When the community is faithful, the material conditions of its life reflect the character of a God whose faithfulness to his promises is as specific and as concrete as the promises themselves. When the community is unfaithful, the material consequences are equally specific — not as arbitrary punishment but as the natural result of a community organizing its life around something other than the character of the God whose presence was the source of its distinctiveness and its flourishing.

The curses of chapter twenty-six reach their most devastating expression in the description of exile — the scattering of Israel among the nations, the desolation of the land in their absence, the humiliation of defeat and captivity. But even within the darkest passage of the curses, the covenant's resilience is asserted: yet in spite of this, when they are in the land of their enemies, I will not reject them or abhor them so as to destroy them completely, breaking my covenant with them. I am the LORD their God. The covenant endures even through the most severe consequences of its violation, because the covenant is grounded not in Israel's faithfulness but in the character of the God who made it. This final word of grace within the curses is the book's most concentrated statement of what the entire sacrificial system has been expressing: that the holy God who requires holiness of his people is the same God who provides the means for their restoration when they fail, and whose commitment to the relationship he has established is not finally defeated by their failure to honor it.

Chapter 6

Where People Get It Wrong

*"Do not think that I have come to abolish the Law or the
Prophets; I have not come to abolish them but to fulfill them."*
— *Matthew 5:17*

Treating Leviticus as Irrelevant to Christians

The most pervasive misreading of Leviticus in Christian contexts
is not a misreading of any specific passage but a wholesale
dismissal of the book's relevance — the assumption that because
the sacrificial system has been superseded by Christ's once-for-all
sacrifice, and because the food laws and purity regulations were
abolished by the New Testament, there is nothing in Leviticus that
a Christian reader needs to engage beyond a general appreciation
of its historical context. On this reading, Leviticus is archaeology
— interesting for understanding where the New Testament came
from, occasionally useful for tracing typological connections
between the Levitical system and Christian theology, but not a text
that makes direct demands on the community that reads it.

This reading misses several things simultaneously. It misses
the fact that the New Testament's own engagement with Leviticus
is far more extensive and more substantive than a typological
reading of the sacrificial system can account for. Jesus quotes
Leviticus nineteen — love your neighbor as yourself — as one of
the two commandments on which all the law and the prophets
hang. Paul quotes the same verse in his letters as the summary of
the entire law. The holiness code's social ethics — its commands
concerning fair wages, honest weights, care for the poor, and the

equal application of justice — run directly into the prophetic tradition and from there into the New Testament's ethics of community life. The book of Hebrews, which engages the Levitical system most directly, does not dismiss its theological logic but develops it as the framework within which the significance of Christ's priestly work can be understood. Leviticus is not the background to the New Testament. It is part of the same sustained theological argument about holiness, atonement, and the character of the God who has called a people to live in his presence.

The dismissal of Leviticus also misses the theological impoverishment that results from it. Communities of faith that have not engaged Leviticus seriously tend to have thin accounts of holiness — accounts that reduce holiness to personal moral virtue without the book's rich sense of holiness as the comprehensive orientation of an entire community's life toward the character of God. They tend to have thin accounts of atonement — accounts that can speak of forgiveness without the book's carefully developed sense of what it costs to maintain a relationship with a holy God and what the provision for maintaining it reveals about the character of the one who provides it. They tend to have thin accounts of sacred time — accounts that acknowledge the importance of worship without the book's sense of the entire calendar of the community's life as itself a theological statement about what the community values and whose presence organizes its existence. Leviticus is not a detour. It is essential reading for any community that wants to understand the theological depth of what it claims.

Reading the Purity Laws as Moral Condemnation

The most damaging misreading of Leviticus's purity system is the one that treats the conditions designated as unclean as evidence of moral failure, divine disfavor, or inherent unworthiness in the people in whom they occur. This misreading has a long and painful history. It has been used to stigmatize women in their menstrual periods as spiritually dangerous. It has been used to treat people with certain physical conditions as religiously inferior. It has been deployed in various forms to exclude from religious community the very people whose conditions Leviticus itself treats as temporary and resolvable — as liturgical states that the book's purification procedures are designed to address, not as permanent moral verdicts on those in whom they occur.

The corrective that Chapter 5 offered bears repeating here with emphasis: impurity in Leviticus is not sin. A woman who has given birth is unclean for a specified period. She has done nothing wrong. Her condition is the natural consequence of the most creative act the human body can perform, and the period of impurity that follows it is not a penalty for that act but a temporary liturgical status that the purification procedure brings to an end. The same is true of every other condition the purity laws address: the skin disease, the bodily discharge, the contact with a corpse. In each case, the impurity is a condition rather than a judgment, and the provision for its resolution is itself a form of grace — the divine specification of a way back to the conditions that make genuine approach to the sanctuary possible.

The practical consequence of this corrective for communities of faith that read Leviticus is the recognition that the purity system cannot be used to justify any arrangement that permanently stigmatizes people on the basis of conditions that the system itself treats as temporary. Every misuse of Leviticus's purity language to create permanent categories of the religiously excluded represents a misreading of the system whose logic it claims to be applying. The system is designed to manage a boundary between states, not to create a permanent class of the unworthy. And the purification procedures are designed to make restoration possible, not to make it difficult. The God of Leviticus

is not a God who uses the purity system to keep people out. He is
a God who provides the purity system so that people can come in.

Reducing Sacrifice to Primitive Superstition

A second common misreading treats the sacrificial system of
Leviticus as a primitive religious practice whose logic is essentially
magical — the attempt to manipulate a divine power through the
offering of valued goods, to secure favorable treatment through
the performance of required rituals, to appease an unpredictable
deity through the regular provision of what he demands. On this
reading, the sacrificial system reflects an early and undeveloped
stage of religious consciousness, one that the prophets of Israel
themselves criticized and that the New Testament supersedes not
only practically but conceptually — not just replacing the specific
practices but revealing that the entire framework in which they
operated was a misunderstanding of the divine nature and the
divine requirements.

This reading misrepresents both the sacrificial system and the
prophetic critique of it. The prophets did not criticize sacrifice as
such. They criticized sacrifice divorced from the covenant
relationship it was designed to express — sacrifice offered by
communities that were simultaneously violating the social ethics
of the holiness code, treating the ritual performance as a substitute
for the genuine orientation of the whole life toward the character
of God that the ritual was meant to embody. When Isaiah declares
that God is weary of burnt offerings and new moon festivals and
solemn assemblies, the critique is not that these practices are
inherently worthless. It is that they have become the cover under
which injustice is practiced and the poor are exploited — that the
ritual form has been retained while the theological substance it
was designed to express has been abandoned. The sacrificial
system as Leviticus conceives it is not primitive superstition. It is a
carefully organized theology of approach to a holy God, grounded

in the conviction that genuine relationship with the divine is possible and that the terms on which it is possible are given by the God who makes them rather than invented by the worshippers who practice them.

The New Testament's engagement with the sacrificial system, particularly in the book of Hebrews, confirms this point. Hebrews does not argue that the Levitical system was a mistake to be corrected. It argues that the system was a shadow pointing toward the substance — that the repeated sacrifices of the Levitical year were anticipating and preparing for the once-for-all sacrifice of the one High Priest who is himself both the offerer and the offering. The relationship between Leviticus and Hebrews is not the relationship between superstition and enlightenment. It is the relationship between promise and fulfillment — between a system whose logic pointed beyond itself and the reality toward which the system was always pointing.

Misreading the Holiness Code as Legalism

The holiness code of chapters seventeen through twenty-seven is one of the most misread sections of Leviticus in both Jewish and Christian contexts. In Christian contexts, it has often been read as the paradigmatic expression of the legalism that the New Testament is designed to correct — a demanding, comprehensive, burdensome system of requirements that defines the relationship with God in terms of behavioral compliance rather than grace, that measures the community's standing before God by the extent of its law-keeping rather than by the character of its relationship with him. On this reading, the holiness code is Exhibit A in the case against law-based religion, and its supersession by the gospel of grace is the most obvious and most welcome feature of the New Testament's advance beyond the Old.

This reading fundamentally misunderstands the theological context in which the holiness code is given. The code does not establish the relationship between God and Israel. It is given within a relationship that has already been established — by the election of the patriarchs, by the exodus, by the covenant at Sinai, by the construction of the tabernacle and the coming of the divine presence into the camp. The commands of the holiness code are not the conditions for entering the covenant. They are the shape of the life that corresponds to a covenant relationship that has already been given by grace. The framework is identical to the framework of the New Testament's ethical teaching: not do these things so that God will love you, but do these things because God has already loved you and because the life that corresponds to that love takes this specific shape. The holiness code is not legalism. It is the specification of what covenant faithfulness looks like in the texture of daily life, given within a relationship whose ground is the gracious initiative of the God who established it.

Misunderstanding the Jubilee as Utopian Fantasy

The Year of Jubilee described in chapter twenty-five is among the most discussed and most dismissed passages in Leviticus. Historians have noted that there is no clear evidence that the Jubilee was ever consistently practiced in ancient Israel — that the economic disruption it would have caused was severe enough that the social systems that would have had to implement it apparently never managed to do so. On the basis of this observation, the Jubilee is often treated as a utopian ideal — an expression of what a perfectly just society would look like that was never practically achievable, interesting as a statement of prophetic values but not something that can be taken seriously as a guide for real economic arrangements in a real world.

This dismissal misses what the Jubilee is actually doing and why its impracticality does not diminish its theological significance. The Jubilee is not primarily a policy proposal. It is a theological declaration embedded in legislative form: the land belongs to God, and therefore no human economic arrangement that treats land as permanently alienable private property can claim divine sanction. The specific mechanism of the Jubilee — the fifty-year reversion of land to original families, the freeing of debt slaves — is the concrete form that this theological declaration takes in the context of ancient Israel's clan-based agricultural economy. The principle it embodies — that the resources of the earth are held in trust rather than owned outright, and that economic arrangements must periodically be corrected in the direction of the original distribution — is a principle whose application takes different forms in different economic contexts but whose theological ground does not change. The Jubilee has not been rendered obsolete by the fact that ancient Israel did not consistently practice it. It has been rendered newly urgent by every economic arrangement in every subsequent era that has treated the concentration of resources in the hands of the few as the natural and permanent order of things.

Collapsing Leviticus into Mere Ritual

A related misreading treats Leviticus as a book whose concern is exclusively ritual — whose regulations govern the external performance of religious practice without any necessary connection to the interior dispositions of those who perform it or the social arrangements of the communities in which they are embedded. On this reading, Leviticus is a manual of religious procedure whose value is primarily historical and whose relevance to contemporary life is limited to whatever typological or allegorical connections can be drawn between its rituals and the realities they are understood to foreshadow. The book's actual content — its specific regulations, its detailed procedures, its precise calibrations of who does what when and how — is not the point. The point is what the content points to.

This reading evacuates the book of the specificity that is, in fact, its most distinctive feature. Leviticus is a book that takes particularity seriously — that specifies not just that Israel should worship but how, not just that Israel should be holy, but what holiness looks like in the specific texture of the kitchen and the bedroom and the field and the marketplace. The book's resistance to generalization is not a limitation to be overcome by reading through the specific to the general. It is a theological conviction to be received: that the relationship between God and his people is not conducted at the level of general principles but at the level of specific practices, and that the God who cares about the precise procedure for offering a burnt offering cares equally about whether the edges of the field have been left for the poor and whether the day laborer has been paid before the sun goes down. Leviticus is not mere ritual. It is the most comprehensive statement in the Torah of what the entire life of a covenant community looks like when it is organized around the character of a holy God.

Reading Leviticus's Demands as Burdens Rather Than Grace

The final and perhaps most consequential misreading of Leviticus is the one that receives its legislation as burden — as the heavy, comprehensive, relentless imposition of requirements by a demanding deity whose satisfaction is the precondition for the community's survival and whose displeasure is the constant threat that organizes the community's religious life. On this reading, Leviticus is the book of an anxious religion — one organized around the fear of getting it wrong rather than the joy of a relationship with the God who has already gotten it right on the community's behalf.

The corrective is to read the sacrificial system not as the community's attempt to manage a dangerous deity but as the deity's own provision for a people who cannot manage the relationship on their own terms. The five types of offering are not requirements invented by Israel to appease a demanding God. They are given by God himself as the means by which genuine approach to his presence is made possible. The purity system is not a gauntlet that must be run before the sanctuary can be approached. It is the divine specification of the conditions under which genuine approach is possible, provided together with the procedures for meeting those conditions when they have been disrupted. The Day of Atonement is not an annual crisis to be survived but an annual gift — the comprehensive, communal, divine provision for the restoration of the relationship that the year's accumulated failures have compromised. The holiness code is not the oppressive enumeration of what God requires before he will tolerate his people. It is the specification of the life that the already-given relationship makes both possible and appropriate — the shape of a community that has been set free to live in correspondence to the character of the God who has set it free. Leviticus, read on its own terms, is not the book of a burdened religion. It is the book of a God who takes the relationship seriously enough to provide everything it requires.

Chapter 7

What It Means for Modern Life

"Love your neighbor as yourself. I am the LORD."
— Leviticus 19:18

Living as a Distinct People

The most fundamental practical implication of Leviticus for modern readers is the one that the holiness command presses most directly: the community that bears the name of the holy God is called to be visibly and consistently different from the communities around it in ways that correspond to the character of the God in whose name that difference is maintained. This call to distinctiveness is not the call to cultural separatism or to the maintenance of religious identity for its own sake. It is the call to embody, in the specific practices and social arrangements of daily life, the character of the God who is holy — and to do so with enough specificity and enough consistency that the difference is actually visible to those outside the community and actually formative for those within it.

The contemporary challenge this poses is real and specific. Communities of faith in the modern Western world inhabit cultures that are sophisticated, pluralistic, and deeply skeptical of claims to distinctiveness that are not grounded in visible and verifiable difference. The assertion that a community is holy — set apart for the purposes of God — carries no weight in a world that has seen too many communities make that claim while reproducing the social arrangements of the surrounding culture without meaningful variation. Leviticus presses the question that the contemporary context makes newly urgent: what does the distinctiveness actually look like in the specific practices of the community's common life? Not in its stated values or its doctrinal commitments, but in the observable texture of how it manages its economic life, treats its vulnerable members, organizes its time, and conducts its internal relationships. The answer Leviticus gives is simultaneously the most demanding and the most concrete in all of Torah: it looks like this, and this, and this — the specific commands of the holiness code enumerated without apology and without softening.

The Sacrificial Logic and Approaching God Today

The sacrificial system of Leviticus is no longer operative in its specific historical form — the Temple has been gone for nearly two thousand years, the Aaronic priesthood has not functioned since its destruction, and neither Jewish nor Christian communities practice the animal sacrifices the book prescribes. But the theological logic that organized the system has not been superseded, and communities of faith that have inherited the New Testament's interpretation of that logic in terms of Christ's priestly work have not thereby escaped the practical implications of what the logic entails.

The sacrificial logic of Leviticus insists that genuine approach to the holy God is both possible and demanding — that the relationship between the community and its God is not maintained automatically or effortlessly but requires the sustained, deliberate, costly engagement that the sacrificial system was designed to organize. The specific mechanism of approach has changed for those who receive the New Testament's interpretation of that mechanism. But the underlying conviction has not: that drawing near to the holy is a serious undertaking whose seriousness corresponds to the character of the one being approached, that the terms of approach are given by God rather than invented by the worshipper, and that the community that treats its access to the divine presence casually — as something to be taken for granted and managed on its own terms — has misunderstood the most fundamental feature of the relationship it claims to inhabit. The sacrificial system's insistence on the precision and costliness of approach is a permanent word to every community that has received the gift of access to God and is at risk of forgetting what the gift cost.

Sacred Time and the Sanctification of the Calendar

The festival calendar of Leviticus twenty-three has direct and underappreciated implications for how communities of faith understand the relationship between sacred and ordinary time. The seven appointed feasts establish a rhythm of return — regular, calendrically fixed occasions on which the community steps back from the ordinary flow of work and commerce to reorient itself around the defining events and the defining relationships that constitute its identity. The Passover returns Israel annually to its founding liberation. The Feast of Tabernacles returns it to the wilderness dependence that God's provision sustained. The Day of Atonement returns it to the most fundamental dynamic of the covenant relationship: the holy God and the not-yet-holy people, and the divine provision that makes the relationship survivable and fruitful for both parties.

The practical implication of the festival calendar for modern communities of faith is a searching question about the actual rhythm of their common life. Not whether they observe the specific Jewish festivals — the New Testament's interpretation of those festivals in terms of their fulfillment in Christ has reshaped what observance looks like for communities that stand on the other side of that fulfillment — but whether the rhythm of the community's common life actually produces the regular return to the defining realities that the festival calendar was designed to organize. A community whose calendar is organized primarily around the rhythms of the surrounding culture — its commercial seasons, its sporting calendar, its cultural events — and secondarily around religious occasions squeezed into the margins of a schedule organized around other centers, has allowed the ordinary to displace the sacred in a way that Leviticus's festival calendar was specifically designed to prevent. The question is not which festivals to observe but whether the community's time is actually organized around the God whose presence gives the community its reason for existing.

The Jubilee and Economic Justice

The Jubilee principle of chapter twenty-five — that the land belongs to God, that all economic arrangements are provisional rather than permanent, and that the periodic restoration of the original distribution is a theological requirement rather than a utopian aspiration — has more direct relevance to contemporary economic life than its ancient Near Eastern specificity might initially suggest. The specific mechanism of the Jubilee belongs to an agrarian economy organized around land ownership in ways that do not translate directly to a post-industrial economy organized around capital, intellectual property, and financial instruments. But the theological principle that organizes the mechanism — that resources are held in trust rather than owned outright, that the concentration of resources is not the natural and permanent order of things, and that economic arrangements must be periodically evaluated against the standard of the God who owns what human economies manage — is a principle that translates across every economic context because it rests on a theological claim about the character of God and the nature of the human community's relationship to the material world.

For modern communities of faith navigating the question of their relationship to economic life, the Jubilee principle presses most directly at the point where the community's actual financial practices meet the theological claims it makes about ownership, generosity, and the purpose of accumulated resources. The community that affirms the theological principle while organizing its own financial life entirely according to the logic of unlimited accumulation and permanent ownership has not yet allowed the principle to reach the level at which it actually makes demands. The Jubilee is not asking communities to implement a specific economic policy. It is asking them to hold their resources with the openness of those who know that what they manage belongs to the God who gave it — and to allow that knowledge to produce the specific, observable, costly practices of generosity and redistribution that genuine stewardship of what belongs to God requires.

The Holiness Code's Social Ethics

The social ethics embedded in the holiness code of Leviticus nineteen are among the most concentrated and most directly applicable passages in the entire book to contemporary community life. The command to leave the edges of fields and fallen fruit for the poor and the foreigner. The prohibition of stealing, lying, and deceptive dealing. The command not to hold back the wages of a hired worker overnight. The prohibition of cursing the deaf and placing obstacles before the blind. The command to judge fairly regardless of the social status of the parties involved. The prohibition of slander and of standing idly by while a neighbor's blood is shed. And then, in the middle of all these specific commands: love your neighbor as yourself. I am the LORD.

The placement of love your neighbor as yourself within this list of specific commands — not as a general principle that precedes the specifics but as a command embedded among them — is itself a theological argument. Love in Leviticus is not a sentiment or a disposition. It is a practice — the specific, observable, costly treatment of the neighbor that the surrounding commands describe. The neighbor whose wages must be paid before sundown, whose produce must be accessible at the field's edge, who must receive fair judgment regardless of his social standing, who must not be slandered or endangered by indifference to his vulnerability — this is the neighbor who must be loved as oneself. The love command and the specific social commands are not two different things. They are one thing, stated twice: once in the specific form that makes the requirement concrete and once in the summary form that names the principle organizing the specifics. Communities of faith that quote the love command while ignoring the specific social commands that Leviticus nineteen places around it have not yet received the command in the form in which it is given.

The Priestly Vocation and Every-Believer Holiness

The New Testament's development of the priestly imagery of Leviticus in terms of the universal priesthood of believers — all who are in Christ are a royal priesthood, a holy nation, a people belonging to God — does not dissolve the specifically priestly calling that Leviticus describes. It extends it. The demands that Leviticus places on the Aaronic priesthood — greater attention to holiness, greater care in the management of the boundaries between sacred and ordinary, greater responsibility for maintaining the conditions that make genuine approach to the holy possible — are now extended to the entire community rather than confined to a specialized caste within it. Every member of the community shares in the priestly vocation of mediating the holy God's presence to the world in which the community is embedded.

The practical implication of this extension is both liberating and demanding. Liberating, because it removes the distinction between a specially holy class whose lives must correspond to the divine presence and an ordinary class whose lives are governed by lower standards. Every member of the community is called to the same holiness, the same care, the same deliberate attention to the conditions that genuine relationship with the holy God requires. Demanding, because the standards that Leviticus applied to the priests — standards that the example of Nadab and Abihu demonstrated were not negotiable — now apply to the entire community. The casualness with which communities of faith sometimes approach the worship, the formation, and the ethical life of their members is not an exercise of Christian freedom. It is an abdication of the priestly vocation that the New Testament extends to every believer on the basis of the Levitical framework it inherits.

The Covenant Frame for Everything

The most important practical contribution Leviticus makes to modern life is not any specific regulation or any particular theme but the frame within which all of its specifics are given: the covenant relationship between the holy God and the people he has called to live in his presence. Every sacrifice, every purity regulation, every festival, every social command, every economic provision in the book is given within this frame, and the frame determines what the specifics mean and what receiving them requires. The regulations of Leviticus are not the requirements of an impersonal law that must be met to avoid punishment. They are the specifications of a relationship that has already been established by grace and that the regulations are designed to sustain.

For modern communities of faith, this covenant frame is the corrective to every reading of Leviticus that produces either the anxious compliance of those who fear what failure to meet the requirements will cost them or the dismissive irrelevance of those who conclude that the requirements no longer apply. The covenant frame insists that both responses have missed the point. The requirements are not the price of the relationship. They are the shape of the life that the relationship makes both possible and appropriate — the specific form that living in correspondence to the character of the holy God takes in the texture of daily community existence. The God who gave these requirements is the same God who said of his people: I will walk among you and be your God, and you will be my people. The regulations of Leviticus are the answer to the question that declaration immediately generates: what does walking with this God look like, in practice, for the people he has chosen to walk with? Leviticus answers the question with unusual specificity, and its answer has not been made irrelevant by the passage of the millennia that separate its original community from the communities that read it today.

Chapter 8

Modern Reflection

*"You are to be holy to me because I, the LORD, am holy, and I
have set you apart from the nations to be my own."*
— Leviticus 20:26

What Leviticus Does to the Reader Over Time

The previous chapter examined what Leviticus makes possible for
modern readers — how its specific teachings on holiness,
atonement, sacred time, and economic justice can function as
practical resources for communities navigating the demands of
covenant life in the contemporary world. This chapter is
concerned with a different and slower question: what Leviticus
does to the reader over time. Not the immediate application of a
regulation to a specific situation, but the formation that happens
when a person or a community engages with the book seriously
and repeatedly across different seasons of life, allowing its
categories to press into the interior of the community's common
existence and reshape the assumptions that organize it from the
inside.

Leviticus is not designed to be read quickly or read once. Its
formation happens through the kind of sustained, repeated
engagement that liturgical communities have always practiced with
it — through the annual cycle of festivals that return the
community to the same texts in the same seasons across multiple
years, through the regular practice of the Sabbath that embeds the
book's theology of time into the weekly rhythm of the
community's life, through the sustained attention to the specific

commands of the holiness code that gradually reorganizes the community's sense of what matters and what the presence of God requires. The reader who approaches Leviticus as a document to be comprehended in a single reading and set aside will find it strange and largely impenetrable. The reader who returns to it across years of community life, bringing the accumulated experience of what holiness costs and what atonement means and what the presence of God requires, will find that the book keeps yielding more than any previous reading has drawn out.

The Distinctive Character of Leviticus's Encounter

Leviticus engages the reader differently from any other book in the Bible, and the difference is formative in its own right. Where the narrative books of Scripture draw the reader forward through story, where the psalms invite the reader into the emotional and spiritual range of the covenant relationship, where the prophets press the reader with the urgency of the divine word applied to specific historical moments, Leviticus places the reader in the position of a community receiving instruction — instruction that is specific, comprehensive, and organized around the conviction that the details matter because the God being approached is genuinely holy and the approach to holiness requires genuine attention to its conditions.

The repetitive structure of Leviticus — the recurring formulas, the repeated specifications, the careful enumeration of case after case — is not a literary deficiency to be endured. It is itself a formative feature of the book. The experience of reading Leviticus is the experience of inhabiting a world in which distinctions matter, in which the difference between this animal and that one, this condition and that one, this procedure and that one, is not arbitrary but reflects a coherent framework organized around the character of a holy God. Sustained engagement with that experience gradually reshapes the reader's sense of what it means to take the relationship with God seriously — away from the vague spirituality that treats religious engagement as primarily a matter of interior disposition and toward the specific, embodied, materially concrete engagement with the divine presence that Leviticus consistently commends.

The Sacrificial System and the Formation of Gratitude

The sacrificial system of Leviticus produces a specific kind of formation in those who engage it seriously: it cultivates a sense of what it costs to maintain a relationship with a holy God, and therefore a sense of what it means that such a relationship has been made possible at all. The five types of offering, taken together, are a comprehensive accounting of what the covenant relationship requires — not as a burden to be resented but as a measure of the seriousness with which the God of Israel takes the relationship he has established. The burnt offering that consumes the entire animal on the altar, reserving nothing for the worshipper, is the sacrificial form of the recognition that approach to the holy God requires giving without remainder. The sin offering and the guilt offering are the sacrificial form of the recognition that failure within the covenant relationship is real and has consequences, and that genuine restoration from failure requires genuine address of what the failure produced.

For communities of faith that have inherited the New Testament's interpretation of the sacrificial system in terms of Christ's once-for-all offering, the formation that sustained engagement with the Levitical system produces is not the anxiety of those who must repeatedly manage their standing before a demanding deity. It is the deepening gratitude of those who understand what the relationship they inhabit required — who have read carefully enough in Leviticus to know what the Day of Atonement addressed annually and what it cost to address it, and who therefore receive the New Testament's claim about the once-for-all nature of Christ's priestly work not as an abstraction but as the resolution of a specific and costly problem that the Levitical system had been keeping in view across the centuries of its practice. Leviticus does not produce anxious religion. Read carefully, it produces profound gratitude — the gratitude of those who know what the relationship cost and who have not forgotten that the cost was paid.

The Holiness Code and the Formation of the Community's Moral Imagination

The holiness code of chapters seventeen through twenty-seven produces its formation not through a single reading but through the cumulative effect of repeated return to its specific commands in the context of real community life. The commands themselves are not difficult to comprehend. What is difficult — and what takes time and honest communal engagement to develop — is the moral imagination that allows their specific requirements to be received not as external impositions but as the natural expression of the character of the community that bears the name of the holy God.

The command to leave the edges of the field unharvested for the poor and the foreigner — a command whose agricultural specificity belongs to a world most modern readers do not inhabit — produces its formation through the question it generates in different economic contexts: what is the equivalent practice in this community's specific situation that embodies the same conviction about the poor's legitimate claim on the community's resources? The command to pay the day laborer before sundown produces its formation through the question it generates about every economic relationship in which the community participates: who bears the risk in this arrangement, and does the distribution of risk correspond to the character of a God who is concerned for the vulnerable? The prohibition of slander and the command to rebuke a neighbor openly rather than nursing resentment produces its formation through the sustained, countercultural practice of direct, honest, loving confrontation within the community rather than the management of relationship through the careful maintenance of impression. Each command is a specific shape that the holiness of God takes in the texture of daily communal life, and the formation that the holiness code produces is the gradual internalization of those shapes as the natural expression of who the community is rather than the external requirements of what the community must perform.

The Day of Atonement and the Formation of Self-Knowledge

The Day of Atonement described in chapter sixteen is the most concentrated instrument of communal self-knowledge that the Levitical calendar provides. The annual return to the rituals of the tenth day of the seventh month — the cessation of work, the fasting, the elaborate priestly procedures that address the accumulated sin and impurity of the entire community and the sanctuary itself — is designed to produce in the community a realistic and honest engagement with the gap between its calling and its performance across the preceding year. Not the managed self-assessment of a community that has decided in advance that its record is acceptable, but the honest, communal, liturgically structured acknowledgment that the year has produced failure as well as faithfulness, compromise as well as covenant fidelity, the accumulation of what needs to be addressed as well as what can be celebrated.

For modern communities of faith that have inherited the Day of Atonement's logic through the New Testament's interpretation of it, the formative dimension of the annual return to honest communal self-assessment has not been superseded. What has changed is the mechanism through which the assessment leads to restoration. What has not changed is the value of the regular, structured, communal practice of honest engagement with the gap between calling and performance — the practice that prevents the community from settling into the self-congratulatory assessment that its record is better than it is, that keeps the community realistic about its need for the restoration that only the one who has entered the holy of holies on its behalf can provide, and that cultivates the quality of corporate humility that the Day of Atonement has always been designed to produce.

The Festivals as Formation Across Generations

The festival calendar of Leviticus twenty-three produces its most significant formation not in the individual reader but in the community that practices it across generations. The Passover meal that the family gathers around annually, the booths that are constructed and inhabited during the Feast of Tabernacles, the solemn assembly of the Day of Atonement — these are not primarily individual spiritual disciplines. They are communal practices whose formation is cumulative and intergenerational, producing in the community that practices them across multiple generations an embodied, experiential knowledge of the events and the relationships they commemorate that no amount of instruction alone can replicate.

The child who grows up in a family that observes the festivals does not primarily learn about the exodus or the wilderness or the Day of Atonement as historical events. She inhabits them — she eats the Passover meal and asks why this night is different from all other nights and receives the answer that shapes her identity before she has the conceptual framework to evaluate it. This is the formation that Leviticus's festival calendar is designed to produce: not the cognitive knowledge of what the events meant but the experiential knowledge of what they mean for the specific community that keeps returning to them as the organizing moments of its year and its identity. Communities of faith that have reduced their sacred calendar to occasional individual observance, disconnected from the rhythmic communal practice that gives the festivals their formative power, have lost something that Leviticus's calendar was specifically designed to preserve.

Failure, Restoration, and the Character of Sustained Reading

Leviticus is realistic about failure in a way that communities of faith have sometimes found easier to acknowledge in principle than to engage in practice. The sin offering and the guilt offering exist because failure within the covenant relationship is expected — not excused, not minimized, but expected and provided for. The Day of Atonement exists because the accumulated failures of a year require a comprehensive annual address that the individual offerings throughout the year do not fully accomplish. The covenant curses of chapter twenty-six exist because the community's capacity for sustained unfaithfulness is as real as its capacity for sustained faithfulness. Leviticus does not pretend that the community called to holiness will achieve holiness without interruption, setback, and the need for restoration. It builds the provision for restoration into the structure of the system as an essential component rather than an afterthought.

The formation this produces in the reader who engages Leviticus seriously over time is a realistic, unsentimental, honest engagement with the community's own patterns of failure — not the paralysis of those who conclude that the gap between calling and performance is too large to bridge, but the steady, persistent, liturgically organized practice of the community that knows how to address its failures because the God who called it to holiness has provided the means for doing so. Leviticus does not produce perfectionism. It produces the kind of community that can name its failures honestly, receive the provision for their address genuinely, and return to the practice of holiness with the resilience of those who know that the covenant relationship is strong enough to sustain their imperfect faithfulness and gracious enough to provide for their inevitable shortfalls. This is the formation that sustained reading of Leviticus produces — not a community that has arrived at holiness, but a community that knows the shape of the life it is called to and keeps returning to that shape with the honest persistence that the covenant relationship both requires and makes possible.

Chapter 9

Reflection Questions

"Consecrate yourselves and be holy, because I am the LORD your God."
— *Leviticus 20:7*

Engaging Leviticus

Leviticus is designed not to be surveyed from a distance but inhabited from within — received not as a historical curiosity about ancient religious practice but as the detailed specification of what life in the presence of a holy God looks like when it is taken seriously. The questions that follow are offered as entry points for that kind of engagement. They are organized around the book's most distinctive themes rather than its narrative sequence, because the themes are what Leviticus is designed to press and because they are the points at which the book most consistently generates the productive discomfort that genuine engagement with a holy God requires. These are not questions with tidy answers. They are questions that grow more demanding the more carefully the book is read and the more honestly the reader brings their own community's life to the encounter. They are designed to be returned to across different seasons of community life, with the expectation that what they yield will change as the community's experience of what holiness costs and what restoration means deepens and becomes more specific.

The goal of these questions is not the completion of a reflection exercise but the kind of honest, sustained, communal engagement with the text that Leviticus itself models in its treatment of the community it addresses. That community was not asked to affirm the general principle of holiness and apply it as they saw fit. It was given specific commands and asked to practice them — to embody the character of a holy God in the specific texture of its specific daily life. The questions that follow press in the same direction: not toward general spiritual principles applied at the community's discretion, but toward the specific, observable, practical implications of the book's most demanding claims for the community that takes them seriously.

On Holiness and the Distinctiveness of the Community

Leviticus's most fundamental command — be holy because I, the LORD your God, am holy — is a call to the kind of visible distinctiveness that corresponds to the character of the God in whose name the distinctiveness is maintained. Before engaging the specific forms that distinctiveness takes, the foundational question must be asked honestly: in what specific, observable ways is your community visibly different from the surrounding culture in ways that correspond to the character of the holy God? Not different in its stated beliefs or its doctrinal commitments, but different in its actual practices — in how it manages its economic life, treats its vulnerable members, organizes its time, and conducts its internal relationships. The answer to this question is a more accurate description of the community's actual holiness than any statement of values can provide.

The holiness code of chapters seventeen through twenty-seven covers domains of life that the surrounding culture also addresses — sexuality, agriculture, economic relationships, legal proceedings, social ethics — and its commands consistently produce a way of life that is different from what the surrounding culture produces in each of those domains. Where is the most significant gap between the shape of life that the holiness code describes and the shape of life that your community actually practices? Not where your community falls short of an impossible ideal, but where the commands of the holiness code are pressing against the actual arrangements of your common life in ways that you have not yet fully received. The gap is not primarily a moral failure. It is information about where the formation that holiness requires is still in progress — where the character of the holy God has not yet fully reorganized the specific practices of the community that bears his name.

The holiness code is addressed to a community, not only to individuals, and many of its commands make no sense as purely individual practices. The field-edge command requires a community with fields. The fair-wages command requires a community with economic relationships between employers and workers. The equal-justice command requires a community with legal and quasi-legal proceedings. Where in your community's common life are there practices — not individual practices but communal ones — that the holiness code directly addresses? And what would it look like for those communal practices to be reorganized in correspondence to the commands the holiness code gives, with the specificity and the consistency that genuine holiness requires rather than the occasional gesture that can be made without disrupting the fundamental organization of the community's life?

On the Sacrificial Logic and Gratitude

The sacrificial system of Leviticus is an accounting of what genuine approach to a holy God requires — not as a burden to be resented but as a measure of the seriousness with which the God of Israel takes the relationship he has established. Before engaging the specific implications of this accounting, the foundational question must be asked: do you receive the provision for approach to God that the New Testament describes as the resolution of a specific and costly problem — the problem that Leviticus has been keeping in view across its twenty-seven chapters — or do you receive it as an abstraction, separated from the specific theological context that gives it its weight and its wonder?

The five types of offering in Leviticus one through seven address five different dimensions of the relationship between the worshipper and God: the comprehensive self-dedication of the burnt offering, the agricultural thanksgiving of the grain offering, the communal celebration of the fellowship offering, the address of inadvertent failure in the sin offering, and the restitution of the guilt offering. Which of these five dimensions of the relationship is most underdeveloped in your own engagement with God? Where is the comprehensive self-dedication most qualified, the gratitude most routine, the communal dimension most individual, the honest address of failure most avoided, the restitution of what has been wrongfully taken most deferred? The five offerings together constitute a comprehensive picture of what genuine engagement with the covenant relationship requires, and the gaps in that picture for any individual or community are the gaps where Leviticus has the most to press.

The Day of Atonement exists because the annual accumulated failures of an entire community require a comprehensive annual address that the individual offerings throughout the year do not fully accomplish. What is your community's equivalent of the Day of Atonement — the regular, structured, communal practice of honest engagement with the gap between its calling and its performance? Not the individual confession that may happen in private, but the communal practice that brings the whole community before the reality of what the year has produced and what needs to be addressed before the next year begins. If your community has no such practice, what would it take to develop one, and what resistance would such a development encounter from those who prefer the accumulated failures to remain unaddressed?

On the Purity System and Honest Self-Examination

The purity system of Leviticus eleven through fifteen manages the boundary between conditions that permit sanctuary approach and conditions that do not — not as a moral judgment on those in whom the relevant conditions occur but as a practical specification of what genuine approach to the holy requires and what temporarily disrupts it. The critical formative question the purity system presses on the modern reader is not about the specific conditions it designates as unclean, most of which do not apply in the forms the book describes. It is about the underlying conviction: that the conditions under which one approaches the holy God matter, and that honest attention to those conditions is itself a form of reverence rather than an obstacle to spontaneous spirituality.

Where in your own engagement with worship and prayer is there the most significant gap between the conditions in which you actually approach God and the conditions in which the approach is most genuinely attentive and most genuinely honest? Not the liturgical conditions that Leviticus specifies — those belong to the specific context of the Levitical system — but the interior conditions: the quality of attention, the honesty about the actual state of the relationship, the willingness to acknowledge what has happened since the last approach before simply proceeding to the next one. Leviticus's insistence that approach to the holy requires genuine attention to the conditions of the approach is a permanent word to every generation that is tempted to treat access to God as a default that requires no particular preparation or honesty.

On the Social Ethics of the Holiness Code

Leviticus nineteen contains within a few verses some of the most concentrated social ethical teaching in the entire Bible: the field-edge command for the poor and the foreigner, the prohibition of theft and deception, the command to pay workers before sundown, the prohibition of cursing the deaf and placing obstacles before the blind, the command to judge fairly regardless of social status, the prohibition of slander and of standing idly by while a neighbor's blood is shed, and then — in the middle of all these specifics — the command to love the neighbor as oneself. Before engaging the specific questions these commands generate, the foundational question must be asked: do you read these commands as addressed to you and your community specifically, in your specific economic and social situation, or do you read them as addressed to ancient Israel in a context too remote from your own to make direct demands?

Take the field-edge command and translate it honestly into the economic context of your community: what resources does your community have access to that the poor and the foreigner have a legitimate claim on, and is that claim being honored in any specific and observable way? Not in principle — in practice. What does the equivalent of leaving the edges of the field unharvested actually look like for a community that does not farm but that manages financial resources, institutional resources, relational networks, and access to opportunity? The command does not apply because the agricultural economy it addressed has changed. It applies because the conviction organizing it — that the resources of the community are not entirely its own, and that the poor and the foreigner have a legitimate claim on what the community has — has not changed.

The command to pay workers before sundown addresses the power differential between employers and workers — the reality that the worker who is not paid on time bears the cost of the employer's delay in a way the employer does not. Where in your community's economic life — or in the economic life of the institutions your community is embedded in — is this power differential being reproduced in ways that the holiness code directly addresses? The question is not whether your community explicitly endorses exploitation. It is whether the specific arrangements of the economic relationships your community participates in correspond to the character of a God who requires that the day laborer be paid before the sun goes down.

On the Festivals and Sacred Time

The festival calendar of Leviticus twenty-three structures the community's year around a set of appointed times whose significance is determined by what God has done rather than by the rhythms of the surrounding culture. The foundational question the festival calendar presses on the modern community is the one about the actual organization of the community's time: what determines the rhythm of your community's common life — the sacred calendar, or the calendar of the surrounding culture? Not whether you observe specific religious occasions, but whether the overall organization of the community's time corresponds to the conviction that the community's life belongs to the God who has called it, or to the conviction that religious occasions are additions to a life whose fundamental organization is determined by other centers.

The Feast of Tabernacles — the seven-day festival during which Israel lived in booths constructed from branches and palm fronds — is the festival whose embodied practice is most directly formative. It is not enough to know about the wilderness wandering that the festival commemorates. The community that inhabits the booth for seven days, sleeping and eating in the construction of branches rather than in the security of a permanent structure, is doing something that the community that merely remembers the wilderness cannot do: it is inhabiting the vulnerability that the wilderness represented, experiencing in its own body the dependence on divine provision that sustained Israel in the desert, and returning from the experience with a knowledge of what the God who provided in the wilderness is like that cannot be acquired through instruction alone. What embodied practices does your community engage in that produce this kind of experiential knowledge of the defining realities of its faith?

On the Jubilee and Economic Imagination

The Year of Jubilee in chapter twenty-five is the most economically ambitious provision in the entire Torah, and the question it most directly presses on modern communities is not the policy question of how to implement a Jubilee in a contemporary economy but the theological question of what the community actually believes about the ownership of the resources it manages. The Jubilee rests on a foundational claim: the land is mine, says the LORD, and you are but aliens and my tenants. Do you actually believe this — not in principle, not as a theological proposition to be affirmed, but in the specific way that would affect the actual financial arrangements of your community if it were genuinely operative? What would change about the way your community manages its financial resources if the conviction that those resources are held in trust rather than owned outright were genuinely operational rather than merely stated?

The Jubilee provision for the release of debt slaves — every fiftieth year, those who have sold themselves into servitude because of debt are freed — addresses the most extreme consequence of the economic vulnerability that the surrounding society produces. Who in your community's social context is in the equivalent of debt servitude — bound by economic arrangements that they cannot exit on their own terms, whose freedom requires a generosity from those with more resources than they have? And what would the Jubilee principle require of your community in relation to those people — not as a policy prescription but as a theological question about what the character of the God who commands the Jubilee looks like in the community that bears his name?

Questions for Continued Engagement

These questions are a beginning rather than an ending. Leviticus is designed to generate more searching engagement the more honestly it is read — not because it is obscure but because its specificity always outruns the general principles the reader is inclined to substitute for it. The reader who returns to Leviticus in a year will find that the questions have not been answered and filed away but have deepened and become more concrete, because the community's experience of what holiness costs and what atonement means has become more specific and because different sections of the holiness code have become newly urgent in light of what the community has encountered in the intervening time.

The most important thing about these questions is not that they be answered definitively but that they be taken seriously with the same quality of specificity that Leviticus itself models. The God who specifies the precise procedure for the burnt offering, who gives exact instructions for what happens on the Day of Atonement, who enumerates the field-edge command and the fair-wages command and the equal-justice command in the same breath as the command to love the neighbor — this God is not satisfied with the general affirmation of the principle. He is asking for the specific practice that the principle requires in the specific community that claims to live in his presence. The questions that Leviticus generates are not questions to be answered at the level of principle. They are questions to be answered at the level of practice — which is the only level at which the holiness Leviticus describes actually exists.

Chapter 10

Five Lessons

*"I will walk among you and be your God, and you will be my
people."*
— *Leviticus 26:12*

Five Lessons from Leviticus

The capacity of Leviticus to form communities of faith has not
diminished across the three millennia since its legislation was first
given. The book that ancient Israel's rabbis considered the most
important text with which children should begin their study of
Torah has proven capable of addressing communities as different
from one another as the Second Temple community that
developed the elaborate priestly institution it describes, the
rabbinic communities that found in its legislation the framework
for a diaspora holiness that did not require a functioning Temple,
the Christian communities that read its sacrificial system as the
theological context for understanding the once-for-all offering of
Jesus, and the diverse communities of faith navigating the
contemporary world. The reason is not that the book is general
enough to mean anything to anyone. It is that the specific claims it
makes about the character of God, the nature of the community
called to live in his presence, and the shape of the life that
corresponds to that calling address dimensions of community
existence that do not change with the century or the culture.

The five lessons that follow are not a summary of Leviticus's
content. They are a distillation of the most persistent and most
demanding things the book asks of those who receive it — the

things that remain pressing after all the historical context has been provided, all the structural features have been explained, all the specific regulations have been examined in their original setting. They are the lessons that remain when the reader has finished absorbing the information the book provides and is left with the question the information has been building toward from the first call to Moses from the tent of meeting: what does it mean to be the community that lives in the presence of the holy God? Each lesson is an answer to that question from a different angle, and together they constitute the response that Leviticus has been pressing its readers toward from its opening sacrifice to its closing declaration of covenant faithfulness.

Lesson One: Holiness Is Comprehensive, Not Compartmental

The first and most foundational lesson of Leviticus is the one that the holiness command states most directly, and the holiness code develops most extensively: holiness in the biblical sense is comprehensive rather than compartmental — it touches every dimension of the community's life rather than being confined to the specifically religious dimensions that most contemporary communities are inclined to designate as sacred. The God who requires holiness of his people is not a deity whose claims are confined to what happens in worship services or in explicitly religious contexts. He is the God whose character sets the standard for how food is prepared, how sexuality is practiced, and how agricultural land is managed, how economic relationships are conducted, how legal proceedings are organized, and how the vulnerable members of the community are treated. The holiness code of chapters seventeen through twenty-seven covers all of this — not as a miscellaneous collection of religious and ethical regulations that happen to have been assembled in the same text, but as a unified vision of the life that corresponds to the character of the holy God whose presence gives the community its identity and its calling.

This first lesson is simultaneously the most liberating and the most demanding claim Leviticus makes. It is liberating because it dissolves the boundary between sacred and secular that has organized much of Western Christianity's engagement with culture and daily life — the boundary that confines God's claims to the explicitly religious domain and leaves the rest of life organized by other principles. Leviticus will not support this boundary. The God who speaks from the tent of meeting speaks about the field edge and the day laborer's wages and the deaf man who must not be cursed with the same authority with which he speaks about the burnt offering and the high priest's vestments. There is no domain of the community's life that the command to be holy does not reach.

It is demanding because the comprehensive reach of the holiness command means that there is no dimension of the community's life that can be held back from the reorganization that genuine holiness requires. The community that is willing to be holy in its worship but not in its economics, or holy in its personal morality but not in its treatment of the foreigner and the poor, has received the command at too low a level to match what the command actually requires. The holiness code's range — from the altar to the field edge to the bedroom to the courtroom — is not an expression of religious overreach. It is the formal expression of the conviction that the God who is genuinely present in the community is genuinely interested in every dimension of the community's common life, and that the community that takes his presence seriously cannot confine its response to the dimensions it finds most manageable.

For contemporary communities of faith, this first lesson generates a specific and searching audit: which domains of the community's common life have been effectively exempted from the holiness command by the working assumption that those domains are organized by principles other than the character of the holy God? Where has the boundary between sacred and secular been drawn in the community's actual practice in ways that Leviticus will not support? Where is the comprehensive reach of the holiness command pressing on arrangements that the community has treated as given — as the natural organization of the community's economic life, or its social life, or its institutional life — that would need to be reorganized if the holiness command were received at the level of specificity that Leviticus consistently maintains? These are not rhetorical questions. They are the practical form that the first lesson of Leviticus takes when it is received seriously rather than acknowledged in principle and deferred in practice.

Lesson Two: Atonement Is God's Provision, Not Human Achievement

The second lesson of Leviticus is the one that the sacrificial system presses most insistently from its opening burnt offering to its Day of Atonement: genuine restoration of the relationship between the holy God and the not-yet-holy people is possible, but it is possible because God has provided the means for it rather than because the community has achieved it through its own resources or its own moral effort. This is among the most counterintuitive and most consistently resisted claims in the entire Torah, because it runs directly against the human instinct to manage the relationship with God through the accumulation of merit — to treat the covenant relationship as fundamentally a performance relationship in which the community's standing before God is determined by the quality of its compliance with the divine requirements.

Leviticus does not support this instinct, and the evidence that it does not is the sacrificial system itself. If the community's relationship with God depended on the community's own achievement of the holiness the book requires, the system would need no provision for failure — or the provision for failure would be the final word, the record of the community's inability to maintain the relationship it had been called to. But the sacrificial system is not the record of failure. It is the divine provision for the restoration of a relationship whose failure has been anticipated and whose restoration has been organized by the God who established the relationship in the first place. The five types of offering are not the community's attempts to recover standing that has been lost. They are the God-given means of maintaining a relationship whose maintenance requires more than the community can provide on its own terms.

The Day of Atonement is the most concentrated expression of this lesson. It is not an annual crisis to be survived by a community desperately trying to meet a standard it has failed all year to maintain. It is an annual gift — the comprehensive, communal, divinely specified provision for the restoration of the relationship that the year's inevitable failures have compromised. Aaron enters the holy of holies not on the community's terms but on God's — wearing the simple linen garments God has specified, performing the rituals God has prescribed, making atonement for the community through means that God has provided rather than means the community has devised. The effectiveness of the Day of Atonement does not depend on the community's penitential intensity or its moral record across the preceding year. It depends on the character of the God who has specified these procedures as the means by which the relationship is reconstituted and who has committed himself to receiving what is offered on those terms.

For communities of faith that have inherited the New Testament's interpretation of this lesson in terms of Christ's once-for-all priestly work, the practical implication has not changed. The relationship with God that the New Testament describes is no more dependent on human moral achievement than the relationship that the Levitical system describes. The community that treats its standing before God as the product of its own spiritual performance — that experiences the relationship as fundamentally dependent on how well it has kept up with its religious obligations — has not yet received the second lesson of Leviticus at the level at which the book presses it. The relationship is given by grace and maintained by the provision that grace has made. The community's response to that grace — its genuine, sustained, costly engagement with the life of holiness — is not what creates the relationship or maintains it. It is what the relationship, already given and already maintained by the God who established it, looks like when it is genuinely inhabited.

Lesson Three: The Community's Life Is the Argument

The third lesson of Leviticus is the one that the holiness code presses most directly in its opening command and most extensively in its twenty-seven chapters of specific regulation: the community of God's people is not primarily an institution that proclaims a message about God but an embodied argument for what God is like — a community whose common life is itself the most powerful and most visible statement available about the character of the holy God in whose presence it lives and in whose name it exists. The command to be holy because I, the LORD your God, am holy is not primarily a command to hold correct beliefs about God's holiness or to make correct statements about it. It is a command to embody it — to live in a way that makes the character of the holy God visible in the specific texture of daily communal life in a way that no proclamation alone can achieve.

This third lesson is one that the entire history of Israel's engagement with the surrounding nations confirms in both its positive and its negative dimensions. When Israel was faithful to the holiness code — when its economic practices reflected the conviction that the land and its resources belonged to God and were to be managed in correspondence to his character, when its legal proceedings reflected the equal justice the holiness code requires, when its treatment of the poor and the foreigner and the vulnerable reflected the concern for the marginal that the holiness code consistently commends — the community was a visible embodiment of what a life organized around the holy God looks like. When Israel was unfaithful — when it reproduced the economic arrangements and the social ethics of the surrounding nations rather than the arrangements and ethics of the holiness code — the argument its life was making about the character of its God was the argument the surrounding nations could have made about their own.

For modern communities of faith, this third lesson generates a question that the surrounding culture's observation of the community is already implicitly answering: what does the watching world conclude about the character of the God this community claims to serve on the basis of the observable arrangements of the community's common life? Not on the basis of its stated beliefs or its public proclamations, but on the basis of the specific, observable, concrete practices of how the community manages its resources, treats its members, conducts its institutional life, and relates to those outside its boundaries. The community whose common life makes the watching world curious — that produces in outside observers the question of why this community is different and what the difference comes from — is the community that has received Leviticus's third lesson at the level of specificity it requires. The community whose common life is indistinguishable from the life of the surrounding culture in every domain that Leviticus touches has not yet received the lesson, whatever it may assert about the importance of holiness in its statements of faith.

The third lesson also carries a specific implication for how communities of faith understand the relationship between proclamation and practice. The temptation to treat proclamation as the primary form of the community's engagement with the world, and practice as the secondary form that ideally supports the proclamation, inverts the priority that Leviticus establishes. The community's life is the argument. Its proclamation is the explanation of the argument. When the life corresponds to the proclamation, the proclamation is credible. When the life does not correspond, the proclamation is undermined — not by the community's failure to proclaim correctly, but by the community's failure to live in a way that makes the proclamation visible. Leviticus's comprehensive specification of what the holy life looks like is not supplementary to the covenant community's mission. It is the community's mission in its most concrete and most demanding form.

Lesson Four: Sacred Time Shapes Sacred People

The fourth lesson of Leviticus is the one that the festival calendar of chapter twenty-three presses most directly: the community that does not organize its time around the sacred calendar of the God who calls it to holiness will find its identity and its character shaped by the calendars of the cultures in which it is embedded rather than by the character of the one in whose name it exists. Time is not a neutral medium through which communities move while being shaped by other forces. It is itself a shaping force — the rhythm of return to the same occasions, the embodied practice of the same commemorations, the regular disruption of ordinary productivity by the sacred appointments of the holy God all produce, over years and generations, a community whose sense of what matters, whose knowledge of what the covenant relationship has been, and whose confidence in what it will be is formed in ways that no amount of explicit instruction can replicate.

The festival calendar of Leviticus accomplishes this formation through a rhythm that is simultaneously annual and lifelong. The annual return to the Passover meal renews the community's identity as the people who were liberated from slavery — not as a historical fact about remote ancestors but as the defining reality of who this people is, enacted again in the meal that makes the liberation present rather than simply remembered. The annual construction and habitation of the Feast of Tabernacles booths renews the community's knowledge of the wilderness dependence that God's provision sustained — not as information about what happened in the desert but as embodied experience of the vulnerability that the God of the covenant met with the specific faithfulness that the feast commemorates. The annual observance of the Day of Atonement renews the community's honest engagement with its own accumulated failure and its confident reception of the restoration that the God of the covenant provides — not as a theological proposition about divine forgiveness but as a communal practice that produces and renews the quality of corporate honesty and corporate trust that the covenant relationship requires.

For modern communities of faith, this fourth lesson generates the most practically demanding question of all: is the community's time actually organized in a way that produces the formation the sacred calendar is designed to generate, or has the rhythm of the surrounding culture — its commercial seasons, its entertainment calendar, its academic and professional schedules — displaced the sacred calendar as the organizing rhythm of the community's common life? The displacement does not happen through a deliberate decision. It happens through the accumulation of small accommodations — the worship service shortened to fit the schedule, the festival moved to a more convenient date, the Sabbath redefined as personal downtime rather than sacred rest — until the rhythm of the community's life is shaped primarily by the culture in which it is embedded and only secondarily, and marginally, by the God whose appointed times are meant to be the organizing rhythm of everything else. The fourth lesson of Leviticus is the insistence that this accumulation of accommodations has consequences — that the community shaped primarily by the culture's calendar will be a culturally shaped community, and that the community shaped primarily by the sacred calendar will be a differently and more distinctively formed people.

Lesson Five: The Covenant Holds Through Failure

The fifth and most pastorally sustaining lesson of Leviticus is the one embedded in the most severe passage of the book — the covenant curses of chapter twenty-six. Even in the description of the most extreme consequences of covenant unfaithfulness — the disease, the drought, the defeat by enemies, and finally the exile and the scattering of the people among the nations — there is a word of grace that refuses to be the final word: yet in spite of this, when they are in the land of their enemies, I will not reject them or abhor them so as to destroy them completely, breaking my covenant with them. I am the LORD their God. The covenant holds. Not because the community has merited its continuation, not because the failure has been minor enough to overlook, but because the character of the God who established the covenant is not finally determined by the character of the community that inhabits it. The covenant holds because of who he is rather than who they are.

This fifth lesson is the one that Leviticus presses most directly against every form of the anxiety that can afflict communities of faith navigating their own patterns of failure and unfaithfulness. The anxiety that the accumulated failures of the community have finally exceeded the capacity of the covenant relationship to sustain them. The anxiety that the gap between the holiness the community is called to and the holiness it actually embodies has become too large for the relationship to bridge. The anxiety that the community has forfeited its standing before the holy God through the specific, documented, communally visible failures that its history contains. Against all of these forms of anxiety, the fifth lesson of Leviticus speaks with unusual directness: the covenant holds. Not because the failures have not been real, but because the God who established the covenant has committed himself to not rejecting the community that inhabits it, even in the midst of the consequences that faithlessness produces.

The practical implication of this lesson is not complacency — the conclusion that failure is without consequence and that the covenant relationship can be treated casually because it will survive anything. The covenant curses of chapter twenty-six exist precisely because failure has real and specific consequences, and the progression of consequences described in the chapter is not a theological fiction. The practical implication is resilience — the capacity of the community to receive the consequences of its failures honestly, to engage the restoration that the covenant provides genuinely, and to return to the practice of holiness with the confidence of those who know that the God who calls them to holiness is the same God who provides the means for their restoration when they fall short of it. This is the formation that Leviticus is designed to produce across the entire arc of its legislation: not a community that has achieved holiness and no longer requires the provision for failure, but a community that knows how to fail honestly, receive restoration genuinely, and return persistently to the shape of the life that corresponds to the character of the God in whose presence it lives.

What Leviticus Has Given to the World

The influence of Leviticus on the history of communities of faith and on the intellectual and moral history of Western civilization is both more extensive and more direct than most modern readers who skip the book have reason to suspect. The sacrificial system that Leviticus describes provided the theological vocabulary within which the earliest Christian communities interpreted the significance of Jesus's death and resurrection — not as the importation of alien categories into an otherwise non-sacrificial understanding of the gospel, but as the fulfillment of the specific theological logic that Leviticus had been developing and that the New Testament received as the framework adequate to the event it was interpreting. The book of Hebrews in particular is incomprehensible without Leviticus — not as a typological curiosity but as a sustained theological argument whose every move depends on the Levitical categories it is developing and extending.

The social ethics embedded in the holiness code have had an influence on the moral development of Western culture that extends far beyond the communities that read Leviticus as Scripture. The command to love the neighbor as oneself, embedded in chapter nineteen and quoted by Jesus and Paul as the summary of the entire law, has organized more of Western moral philosophy than most secular moral philosophers are inclined to acknowledge. The concern for the poor and the foreigner that runs through the holiness code has animated more social reform movements — from the medieval church's engagement with poverty to the abolitionist movement to twentieth-century civil rights advocacy — than the explicitly secular versions of those movements's histories typically acknowledge. The Jubilee principle has provided the theological grounding for every serious Christian engagement with the question of economic justice, from the liberation theology of the twentieth century to the contemporary discussions of debt relief and restorative economics.

This influence does not mean that communities formed under Leviticus's direct or indirect influence have been consistently faithful to its vision. The community that has read love your neighbor as yourself for three millennia has also, repeatedly and consequentially, failed to embody the specific social commands that Leviticus nineteen places around it. The community that has affirmed the Jubilee principle has rarely

practiced anything resembling the Jubilee's actual requirements.
The community that has insisted on the comprehensive reach of
the holiness command has repeatedly drawn the boundary
between sacred and secular in ways that Leviticus will not support.
Acknowledging this history is not a reason to abandon Leviticus.
It is a reason to read it more carefully and more honestly — to
allow the book's specificity to press against the comfortable
generalities in which its most demanding claims have been
domesticated across the centuries.

The Enduring Questions

The questions that Leviticus raises cannot be finally answered by
any community in any era, and they will therefore continue to
press themselves on every community that takes the book
seriously. They are questions about the comprehensive reach of
the holiness command — whether the community's life in every
domain corresponds to the character of the holy God or whether
there are domains that have been effectively exempted from his
claims. They are questions about the community's relationship to
its own failure — whether it engages that failure honestly and
receives the restoration that the covenant provides genuinely, or
whether it manages the gap between calling and performance
through the maintenance of appearances. They are questions
about the organization of the community's time — whether the
sacred calendar or the cultural calendar shapes the community's
life more fundamentally and what that reveals about where the
community's actual center of gravity lies.

These questions are currently being asked with unusual
urgency in the contemporary world, because the communities that
previously provided frameworks for identity, moral formation,
and the organization of life around something larger than private
accumulation have eroded significantly, and the hunger for a
community whose common life actually corresponds to the values

it proclaims is everywhere evident. Leviticus's response to this condition is the same response it has always offered: here is the character of the holy God in whose presence you are called to live; here is the specific shape that a community organized around that character takes in the texture of its daily existence; here is the provision for the failures that are inevitable and the restoration that makes return to the holy life possible. Come and receive the instruction. Come and practice the holiness. Come and discover that the life organized around the presence of the holy God is, as Leviticus has been insisting from its first call to Moses to its final word of covenant faithfulness, the only life adequate to what human communities are made for.

The Character of Sustained Reading

Reading Leviticus well over a lifetime — or across the life of a community — requires habits of engagement that do not develop without the sustained, repeated return to the text that the book's own festival calendar was designed to organize. The most important is the habit of receiving the book's specificity as a gift rather than an obstacle — of allowing the detailed, particular, materially concrete commands of the holiness code to press on the specific, particular, materially concrete arrangements of the community's actual life rather than translating them into general principles that make no specific demands on anything specific. Leviticus is not a book of principles. It is a book of practices — specific practices given to a specific community organized around the presence of a specific God, and whose specificity is the formal expression of the conviction that the relationship with that God is too serious to be conducted at the level of generality.

The community that reads Leviticus well across years and generations will find that different sections of the book press most urgently at different stages of the community's life. The sacrificial system will press most urgently in seasons when the community is navigating its own failure and needs to receive the provision for restoration honestly rather than managing the failure through performance. The holiness code will press most urgently when the community is deciding how to organize its economic relationships, its social practices, its institutional arrangements — pressing the question of whether those arrangements correspond to the character of the holy God or to the character of the surrounding culture. The festival calendar will press most urgently when the community is navigating the temptation to allow the rhythm of the culture to displace the rhythm of the sacred appointments that are meant to organize its life. The covenant blessings and curses will press most urgently when the community is navigating the consequences of past unfaithfulness and needs to hear both the honest assessment of what unfaithfulness produces and the word of grace that refuses to be the final word about the community the covenant sustains.

The Permanent Invitation

The invitation that Leviticus extends across its twenty-seven chapters is the invitation that the LORD's first word to Moses from the newly completed tabernacle announces and that the covenant declaration of chapter twenty-six confirms: come and live in the presence of the holy God, and let the character of that presence reorganize every dimension of the community's life in correspondence to the character of the one whose presence gives the community its identity and its calling. It is an invitation addressed to a community that is not yet holy, that will fail repeatedly in the course of trying to be, and that will need the provision for failure that the book carefully specifies. It is an invitation that does not pretend the community is more than it is or require it to be more than it can be before the invitation is extended.

Leviticus was not written for a community that had already achieved the holiness it describes. It was written for a community at the threshold — camped at the foot of a mountain, organized around a newly constructed sanctuary, receiving instruction for a way of life whose full conditions had not yet been established, navigating the daily practical question of what the presence of the holy God required of them in the circumstances they were actually in. That situation is, in its essential features, the situation of every community of faith in every subsequent era that has taken the invitation seriously. The conditions change. The specific mechanisms by which the invitation is received and the holiness it calls for is practiced change with them. But the invitation is the same, and the character of the God who extends it is the same, and the life that genuine reception of the invitation produces is, as Leviticus has been insisting from its first word to its last, the life that the God who walks among his people and is their God has made both possible and worth the cost of pursuing.

Closing Reflection

"I will walk among you and be your God, and you will be my
people. I am the LORD your God, who brought you out of Egypt
so that you would no longer be slaves."
— Leviticus 26:12-13

Leviticus has endured because the question it answers does not change. How does a people that is not holy live in the presence of a God who is? Every generation of the community that bears the name of the holy God has faced this question in its own specific circumstances, with its own specific failures and its own specific needs for the restoration that the covenant provides. The specific mechanisms by which the question was answered in the wilderness camp at Sinai — the burnt offerings and the sin offerings, the priestly mediations and the purity procedures, the Day of Atonement and the festival calendar — no longer function in the form the book describes. But the question those mechanisms were answering is as urgent as it has ever been, and the theological convictions that organized them — about the character of the holy God, the nature of the community called to live in his presence, and the provision he has made for the failures that proximity to holiness inevitably reveals — remain the convictions that every subsequent generation must receive and inhabit if it is to answer the question with the seriousness it deserves.

What gives Leviticus its lasting power is not the drama of its narratives, of which it has almost none. It is not the beauty of its poetry, which it largely does not contain. It is the uncompromising seriousness with which it takes the presence of the holy God as the organizing reality of the community's entire existence — a seriousness that refuses to confine the implications of that presence to the specifically religious dimensions of the community's life and insists on pressing them into the kitchen and the field and the courtroom and the marketplace and the bedroom. The God of Leviticus is not a deity whose claims are manageable within the domain of explicit religious practice. He is the God whose holiness is the standard for the whole of life, whose presence in the community changes everything about what the community's life must look like, and whose provision for the community's inevitable failures is as specific and as concrete as his requirements for the life he is calling it to.

One of the most characteristic features of Leviticus, observed across the entire history of its reception by communities of faith in every era and every cultural context, is its resistance to being received at the level of general spiritual principle. Every misreading of Leviticus is a misreading that has substituted a general principle for the specific practice the book requires — that has affirmed the holiness command in principle while exempting some domain of the community's life from its reach, that has acknowledged the importance of atonement while reducing it to a theological category rather than receiving it as the specific divine provision for the specific gap between the community's condition and the holy God's requirements, that has celebrated the Jubilee as an inspiring vision while declining to ask what the Jubilee principle requires of the community's actual financial arrangements. Leviticus does not permit these substitutions. Its insistence on the specific, the concrete, and the practically demanding is not a literary deficiency to be compensated for by the reader's ability to extract the general principle from the particular command. It is the book's most fundamental theological claim: that the relationship with the holy God is conducted at the level of specific practice, not general intention, and that the community that genuinely inhabits the relationship will find it reorganizing every dimension of its specific common life.

Reading Leviticus well over a lifetime — or across the life of a community — produces a formation that cannot be achieved in any other way. Not the mastery of ancient Near Eastern sacrificial systems or the comprehensive understanding of the priestly theology the book develops, but the gradual internalization of the book's most fundamental conviction: that the holy God who walks among his people and is their God takes the relationship seriously enough to specify what it requires and gracious enough to provide what the specification demands of a people who cannot meet it on their own terms. The community that has been formed by sustained, honest, repeated engagement with Leviticus will find that its sense of what holiness means has deepened from the vague aspiration toward moral excellence into something more specific and more demanding — the comprehensive orientation of the entire community's life toward the character of the God in whose presence it lives. And it will find that its sense of what grace means has deepened correspondingly — from the general assurance of divine goodwill into something more specific and more sustaining: the provision of a God who anticipated the community's failure, organized the means for its restoration, and committed himself to not rejecting the people he has called even in the midst of the consequences that their unfaithfulness produces.

The invitation Leviticus extends is the same invitation it has always extended, from the first call to Moses from the tent of meeting to the final word of covenant faithfulness that closes the book's twenty-seventh chapter. Come and receive the instruction. Come and practice the holiness. Come and find that the life organized around the presence of the holy God — specific, demanding, costly, and sustained by a grace that provides everything the relationship requires — is the life that the community called by his name was made for. The holy God who walks among his people is walking still, and the people who are willing to organize their entire common life around the character of his presence are the people that Leviticus has always been written for. They are the people that every generation of the community that bears his name is called to become.

The Bible for Modern Life Series

This book is part of **The Bible for Modern Life** series—an ongoing collection that explores the meaning, historical setting, and message of individual books of Scripture.

Each volume looks closely at the biblical text to help readers understand what it meant in its original context and how its truths still apply to life today.

The goal is simple: to help modern readers engage more deeply with the Bible—one book at a time.

— Samuel Whitaker